17.50

Industry Acclaim for
THE RECRUITER'S ALMANAC and
SHUT UP & MAKE MORE MONEY

"Right on target! The Recruiter's Almanac is readable, reliable, rational and respectable!"

--- Robert O. Snelling, Chairman
Snelling & Snelling, Inc.

*

"'Must' reading for everyone in our business. Insightful and informative, The Recruiter's Almanac is the best instructional manual of its kind!"

--- H. Brent Sanders, Vice President
Chase Adams, Inc.

*

"Radin's scripts are exemplary and funny...jolly good for providing a simple framework of ideas."

--- Angela Mason, CPC
Staffing Industry Report

*

"No office should be without The Recruiter's Almanac --- a perfect complement to Billing Power!"

--- Terry Petra, CPC
International Speaker/Trainer

*

"A breath of fresh air! Shut Up & Make More Money can help turn rookies into pros and pros into star performers!"

--- Bill Vick, President
Vick & Associates

*

"Shut Up & Make More Money is a strongly recommended addition to your training bookshelf."

--- Paul Hawkinson, Publisher
The Fordyce Letter

*

"A rifle shot of crisp, sound advice from a steady, experienced hand."

--- David Lord, Editor
Executive Recruiter News

D1736866

Books by Bill Radin

The Recruiter's Almanac
of Scripts, Rebuttals and Closes
Innovative Consulting, Inc., 1998

Shut Up & Make More Money!
The Recruiter's Guide to
Talking Less and Billing More
Innovative Consulting, Inc., 1995

The Sales Rep Navigator
How to Find the Perfect Sales Rep or
Distributor for Your Business
Innovative Consulting, Inc., 1995

Breakaway Careers
The Self-Employment Resource for
Freelancers, Consultants and Corporate Refugees
Career Press, 1994

Take This Job and Leave It
How to Get Out of a Job You Hate
and Into a Job You Love
Career Press, 1993

BILLING POWER!

The Recruiter's Guide To Peak Performance

By **Bill Radin**

©1995 Innovative Consulting, Inc.
5769 Eaglesridge Lane
Cincinnati, Ohio 45230
(800) 837-7224

BILLING POWER!

The Recruiter's Guide To Peak Performance

By Bill Radin

©1995 Innovative Consulting, Inc.
5769 Eaglesridge Lane
Cincinnati, Ohio 45230
Phone: (800) 837-7224 • Fax: (513) 624-7502
Email: billradin@aol.com • Web site: www.billradin.com

ISBN 0-9626147-4-2 $49.95 Softcover
Library of Congress Catalog Card Number 90-81180
Cover photo: Terry Lynch
Additional photos: Bill Radin
Cover design: Anthony d'Agostino
Printing: BookCrafters, Chelsea, Michigan

10 9 8 7 6 5 4 3

Manufactured in the United States of America

Acknowledgments

The author wishes to thank all the people who have been instrumental in helping make *Billing Power!* a reality, including his family; plus the dedicated and inspired professionals throughout the industry; and especially, Mike Schulman, Bob and Larry Cowan, Jeff Weiss, Toni Jenkins, Terri Rich, Carolyn Barnes, Ron Farnham, Michael Zatzick, Jim Henry, Don Dreifus, Ted Lawson, Margaret Zito, Terry White, Larry Ainsworth, Adrienne Kasower, John Winner, Rima Cohn, Stephanie Quint, Gwen Sabo, Tollis Pompeo, Mark Ouchi, Rona Schneider, Bill LaPerch, Loren Williams, Mark Lebowitz, Paul Hawkinson, Sandy Pogan, David Lord, Joe McCullough, Tom Kelty, Dennis Straw, Ed Marshall, Joe Mehl, Tracy McMullen, Jim Murphy, Kathy Scheiss, Sandra Seta, Sandy Bell, and countless others.

Special thanks to Ron Boustead, Ruth Rivin, Kate Costlow, Ken Kresge, Thea Temple, Joe Ziomek, Diann Cox, James Ferguson, Dr. Chris Dacey, Marc Wolfley, John Nelson, Don Aren, Jim Kennedy, Dan Poynter, Bill Gwynne, Harriet and Ben Kaufman, and Ray Sevin.

Billing Power! is dedicated to Duke Miller.

Table of Contents

Table of Contents

Illustrations and Forms

Introduction

*T*his is a book about the most fascinating and gratifying profession in the world, and how you can learn to be more successful at it.

The personnel placement business offers you the opportunity to change people's lives for the better, by helping them fulfill their occupational dreams.

Job candidates trust you to upgrade their sense of accomplishment, increase their earnings, and improve the quality of their personal and professional relationships.

Your service also enables companies to grow and prosper, and become more competitive on a local, national, and even international level.

In addition, a career in executive search empowers you to fully develop your entrepreneurial skills, while allowing you complete control over your time, methods, and market.

Finally, recruiting can provide you with an outstanding level of personal income, in a relatively short period of time.

How many professions can give you this kind of responsibility, satisfaction, and financial reward?

The Problem

Unfortunately, not all account executives in the personnel placement business are as productive as they'd like to be.

For one reason or another, they are working below their potential, both in terms of personal income, and job satisfaction.

Billing Power! can change all that.

This book introduces you to a new perspective on our business, and gives you the means to improve your productivity.

This carefully tested and innovative method combines the most successful placement strategies in our industry with an effective, client-centered selling technology. Over the years, it has helped increase the billings of account executives across the United States by millions of dollars.

Billing Power! can be put to use immediately, regardless of your desk specialty or geographic location; and it will help you quickly improve the fundamental skills you need to reach your full potential, in terms of earnings, job satisfaction, and ultimately, your beneficial service to others.

Best of all, the *Billing Power!* method will help you increase your production in a manner consistent with your *own* beliefs, personality, and identity.

That's because the *Billing Power!* program respects your integrity and that of your customer. And it recognizes that your success is directly proportional to the rapport you build with others. For that reason, you won't be asked to assume the persona of anyone else; nor create adversarial relationships by the indiscriminate use of inflexible pitches, rebuttals, or closes.

By studying the *Billing Power!* strategies and putting them into action, you can begin to work at your full potential, while maintaining your own unique identity.

Contingency or Retainer?

According to the National Association of Personnel Services (NAPS) in Alexandria, Virginia, there are an estimated eighty thousand recruiters in the United States.

The overwhelming majority are those who charge their clients only for completed search assignments.

Billing Power! specifically addresses the needs of this group (known as "contingency" recruiters), although many of the concepts and techniques will also apply to those who work closely with client companies on a "retained" basis.

As our society becomes more information, or *service* oriented, the need for talented employees with specialized skills has become more acute.

Add to this the changing demographics of a "baby bust" economy, plus the increasing emphasis on job satisfaction and career mobility, and you will quickly see why the personnel placement industry continues to grow.

This growth has brought with it competition, not only from among our ranks, but from many of our client companies who want to attract talent by using their own methods. It is not uncommon for companies to pay "bounties" to their employees who make referrals, or hire permanent, full time staff recruiters to try to do our work.

Competition by itself is nothing to be afraid of. In fact, competition is the sign of a healthy demand. Frankly, I'd begin to *worry* if there was no competition.

The best way to keep up with or beat the competition is to provide a better, more valuable service. This will result in a greater level of job satisfaction, and higher earnings for you. And that's the aim of *Billing Power!*

A Word About Terminology

Every recruiter or placement company has its own language. For example, what do we call ourselves?

I've used the term "account executive" for years, but you may prefer any of the other common titles, such as placement counselor, consultant, executive recruiter, search specialist, or headhunter.

The people we place are usually called candidates, although I find the word "applicant" has a nice ring to it.

The people who pay our fees are referred to as clients, client companies, accounts, or employers.

Search assignments are almost universally known as "job orders," interviews that we arrange are "sendouts," and placements are often called "deals."

The fees we charge our clients for making placements are cumulatively known as "billings."

The more placements we make, the more billings we generate.

The more we bill, the more we earn for ourselves, and the greater the service we render to our candidates and clients.

Another term used in *Billing Power!* is the pronoun "he."

"He" will replace "he/she," and "him" will replace "him/her," and so forth.

Although this type of grammatical usage is anything but politically correct, it's simply done for the reader's convenience, and doesn't mean to imply that all the people in the world are male.

1

The Power of Perception

$\mathcal{W}$ouldn't you agree that the way you look at your business has a powerful impact on your ability to succeed?

When I first applied for a job as an executive recruiter, I knew absolutely nothing about the corporate facts of life. At thirty-three years of age, I had never worked at a conventional job, or collected a regular paycheck.

The nearly fifteen years I had spent as a jazz musician were a lot of fun.

But unfortunately, fun doesn't pay the rent.

You may not be aware of this, but jazz musicians don't make a lot of money.

I mean, the bottom line of my annual tax returns looked like the asking price of a used Hyundai.

One year, I crossed into the unthinkable stratosphere of the five figure income. I was so happy, I thought I'd died and gone to heaven!

I was so poor, I couldn't even afford furniture from Goodwill. I had to collect whatever I could find on the street, and haul it up to my apartment.

To make matters worse, I had accumulated over $20,000 in debt from attending graduate school at the University of Southern California.

Clearly, a career change was in order!

The Interview

Somehow, I heard about the personnel placement business.

I didn't have any great career expectations; executive recruiting just seemed like an interesting way to make a living and help other people. Besides, I needed a job.

So I answered an ad, and went to an interview.

As I shook hands with Jim Smith, the owner/manager of a search firm in Los Angeles, I was immediately impressed by his clean, fancy office and polite, businesslike demeanor.

Hey, this looks all right, I thought.

"Have a seat," said Mr. Smith, "and tell me about yourself."

As I launched into my narrative, Mr. Smith listened patiently, occasionally nodding his head and gazing at my resume.

He must have written me off somewhere in the first sixty seconds of the interview; there was no way I could hide the fact that the only business experience I had was in high school, selling ladies' shoes.

After asking a few perfunctory questions, Mr. Smith stood up and thanked me for coming in.

Rats, I blew it.

"I'll get back with you in a few days," he said, motioning

me toward the door.

Sharing a Trade Secret

Well, he never did get back to me, but he did leave me with a concept that was to shape my perception of the search business for many months to come.

At some point during our brief meeting, he had leaned forward, as if to share a trade secret.

"Just remember," he half whispered. "This business can be summed up in one sentence:

"Executive search is simple in concept, and difficult in execution."

What an interesting way to look at the business, I thought. *I'll remember that.*

Famous Last Words

Although I never heard from Mr. Smith again, everything turned out all right.

I eventually landed a job across the street, working for Mr. Smith's direct competitor. And I did well.

Within a year and a half, I had billed over a quarter million dollars and had become a technical department manager and director of advanced training for the largest search firm in California.

But it wasn't easy. I not only had to learn the ropes of technical recruiting, I had Mr. Smith and his proverbial wisdom to overcome.

For despite a fairly promising start in the business, my desk soon drifted into the Death Valley of deals. The placements which had come so easily in the beginning started to drift beyond my grasp.

As the months dragged on, my lack of billings drained my bank account and began to affect my confidence.

I was in a serious slump, and I wanted to know why.

By observing the attitudes of those around me, I slowly started to notice an amazing phenomenon: the account executives (including myself) who thought of the search business as "simple in concept and difficult in execution" *consistently produced mediocre results!*

Could Mr. Smith be wrong? I wondered. *Maybe there's another way to look at this business!*

The Discovery

From that moment on, I began the quest for a secret recruiting philosophy that would reverse my fortunes and forever prevent me from wandering into the billing desert again.

Finally, after months of observing and interviewing top-producing recruiters, attending seminars, and absorbing the material contained in countless books and tapes, I discovered the deceptively simple clue to high billing.

And fittingly, my success in the business began the moment I discarded Mr. Smith's trade secret and adopted my own:

*The search business is as
simple in concept
as it is in execution!*

Furthermore,

*The more strongly formed and
fundamentally sound your concept,
the better results
your execution will produce!*

For example, let's suppose an urgent matter requires you to travel to Los Angeles, a city you have never visited, and that on arrival, you must pick up a rental car and drive from the airport to Beverly Hills.

Assuming you know how to drive a car and have an accurate map, the trek should take less than twenty minutes. With a clear set of directions (concept), and the ability to operate a vehicle, the trip (execution) is a snap.

Difficulty in execution occurs if you have no directions and no map! Without any visible landmarks and fifty thousand miles of freeway in every direction, it's very possible to drive for hours and get no closer to your destination.

Recruiting is much the same as taking a drive across town. The execution is darned near impossible if you don't know what to do or where you're going.

The Law of Recruiting

Billing Power! is designed to help give your *career* a direction, by introducing you to some new ideas, and helping you learn to apply them.

Everything in this book is supported by a simple underlying concept, which years of experience and millions of dollars in billings have shown to be fundamentally sound.

It's called the Law of Recruiting, and it states that:

> *Successful recruiting comes from*
> *the commitment to satisfy*
> *the employment needs of others*
> *through an aggressive, relentless*
> *process of discovery.*

As long as the Law of Recruiting remains constant, your

ability to help people get what they want will be directly proportional to your success.

Throughout this book, we'll examine ways in which you can increase your productivity by applying this law.

But first, let's take a hard look at the service we provide.

2

Maximizing the Value of Your Service

*L*et me ask you a question: What do your clients pay you to do?

If you answered that you earn your fee by referring qualified applicants, or checking references, or scheduling interviews, or negotiating compensation, you're right.

These are some of your *activities*.

But how would you describe your *service*?

When you think about it, does referring an applicant warrant a $10,000 fee? Does checking a reference lead to a placement? Does scheduling an interview translate into long term employment?   Hardly.

Search and Placement: A Three-Phase Process

We earn our fee by providing our clients with a comprehensive service, which occurs in three distinct, sequential phases: *recruit, offer and transition.*

This approach to the business broadens the scope of your service beyond mere matchmaking.

In fact, to complete the analogy, you might think of your service in terms of matchmaking, performing the wedding ceremony, and acting as a marriage counselor!

Let's take a look at the three phases in more depth.

1] The *recruit* phase is the period in which we write the job order, present applicants to employers, arrange first and second interviews, and thoroughly debrief both parties.

During this phase we're continually clarifying our understanding of our applicants' motivations and needs. We also strengthen our partnership with the client company.

By presenting applicants, we can fine tune our knowledge about the client's hiring needs, likes and dislikes, and current search status. We can also pick up additional information about the company's hiring procedures, benefits, and operation.

2] The *offer* phase begins when the applicant and employer show serious interest in each other. During this phase, we work behind the scenes to put together an acceptable offer.

By this time, we've already made it clear to both parties that *unacceptable* offers will not be presented. Just to play it safe, any other contenders we've presented for the same position now assume "backup" status.

After the offer has been officially accepted, a starting date for employment with the new company is set. In addition, a *position title* and *starting salary* are confirmed.

3] The *transition* phase occurs immediately after the offer is accepted, and continues through the start date, for at least six months into the placed applicant's new job.

This period of "emotional limbo" is when the applicant must resign from his present job, decline a counteroffer attempt, start a new job, take on new responsibilities, and learn to work with a new group of people.

During the transition phase, we must constantly monitor the progress of the applicant, and check with the new employer for his observations.

Their ability to communicate within the first few weeks is essential to laying the foundation for a successful, productive working relationship. Furthermore, the need for our involvement during this period cannot be overlooked.

Executive Search and Rescue

For example, John was a technical writer I placed with a high tech client company in California. Three weeks after John started in his new position, I called to ask him how everything was going.

"Fine," he answered. "They love me here. I've completed the documentation on everything they've assigned me."

Later that day, I placed a call to the hiring manager, expecting him to heap praise on me for my recruiting genius. Boy, was I in for a surprise!

"Bill, I'm afraid I have some bad news for you," said the manager. "I'm going to fire John this afternoon. It looks like we'll have to start the search all over again."

"Really?" I wheezed. "What seems to be the problem?"

"John hasn't produced any of the documentation we need for our customers, and we have to get the work done to meet our deadline. If John can't do it, I'll have to find someone who can."

"Mr. Employer," I said, "this sounds kind of strange to me, since I talked to John this morning and he's under the impression that the documentation he's producing is exactly what you asked for.

"When was the last time the two of you sat down to discuss his assignment?"

"Oh gosh," replied the manager, "it must have been about three weeks ago, right after he started to work here."

"Well then, Mr. Employer," I said, "the two of you should probably talk this through, because there's obviously been a communication breakdown. As far as John is concerned, he's doing a terrific job based on his perception of the assignment."

A simple failure to communicate the task clearly in the beginning had almost resulted in John's termination three weeks later!

Fortunately, we were all able to dodge a bullet. After my call to the employer, the two of them got together to discuss the project. The assignment was quickly clarified, and John went on to finish the documentation needed to meet the deadline.

Clearly, my follow-up during the transition phase saved the deal!

Selling a Value-Added Service

In our profession, we tend to focus so much attention on *recruiting* (the most visible part of our work), that we often fail to recognize and sell the full scope of our service.

The next time an employer says, "That's all right, you just find me the people and I'll do the rest," remind him of your ability and commitment to produce acceptable *offers* and provide for a smooth *transition*.

Presenting the three-phase approach as a value-added service to employers is one of the most powerful selling techniques at your disposal, especially at the time a job order is written. Here are some reasons why:

- The three-phase approach *establishes credibility*. Employers feel comfortable dealing with a professional who knows how the placement process works and can clearly explain his service.

- The three-phase approach *builds value*. "Mr. Employer, I can provide a comprehensive service which goes far beyond simply recruiting applicants. Wouldn't that be to your advantage?"

I once had an employer ask me how much this additional comprehensive service would cost. He was delighted to know that he got all the "extra work" free of charge!

- The three-phase concept distinguishes you from your competition, and clarifies *your service*. "Other firms only work in the 'recruit' phase, Mr. Employer. I work in all three."

27

- The three-phase approach prepares the employer for a predictable sequence of events. This type of preparation is known as "preframing."

Preframing your actions gives the employer the opportunity to express any questions or concerns he may have *before* your work begins. By handling concerns *in advance,* you eliminate potential problems or misunderstandings which may occur later.

- Finally, an explanation of your methodology helps establish a feeling of partnership with the employer, and builds trust. "When we get to the offer stage, Mr. Employer, I'm going to need your help. So tell me now: Can I count on you?"

Try thinking of recruiting as a three-phase process, and remember that

Maximizing the value of your service will increase your billings.

3

Understanding Your Applicants

*M*eet Frank.

Frank is an account executive who works in an office like yours.

Frank is facing a dilemma.

It seems he presented his client's offer to an applicant.

Frank thought the applicant was "in the bag."

That was on Monday.

It seems the applicant wanted to "think it over."

Now Frank is sitting in his manager's office, along with the general manager and the office manager.

It's six o'clock Friday evening, and the applicant hasn't returned Frank's phone calls for four days.

Frank is worried.

Frank's client is worried.

And Frank's manager is worried. So he rounded up all the heavy hitters in the office to brainstorm a deal.

A Meeting of the Minds

"I can't understand it," groans Frank. "He has the *perfect* background for the job!"

"So why the heck can't he make up his mind?" demands the general manager.

"I'm not sure. We got him a ten percent increase in salary, and even threw in three weeks vacation," replies Frank, scratching his head.

"Well, you just haven't *sold* him hard enough," snaps the GM.

"Right! Sell him on the opportunity," growls Frank's manager, as he mashes out his cigarette. "Let him know what a fool he is if he lets this job slip through his fingers!"

"I'll bet if I can just get the applicant more money, he'll take the job," whines Frank, unconvincingly. "Maybe I should call the employer right now and see what he says..."

"Wait a minute, I've got an idea," chimes in the office manager. "Have the employer call the applicant's wife. She's the *real* decision maker!"

"Right! She's the reason he turned down the offer we had for him two months ago," reflects Frank's manager. "How did we handle it then?"

"I think we played take-away. Or did we use the Ben Franklin close? I can't remember..."

What's Wrong with This Picture?

If I were Frank, I'd have a lot to worry about.

Aside from the tactical error he made by presenting an offer to a reluctant applicant, Frank failed to understand the applicant's true needs.

He thought that because the applicant had the "perfect background" for the job, the deal was in the bag.

I used to make the same mistake as Frank, trying to satisfy my *own* needs, rather than those of the applicant.

Then I discovered a method of understanding applicants, and *their* needs.

Once I understood their needs, I could predict with reasonable certainty which applicants were worthy of my time, and which deals were likely to close.

Naturally, my billings rose as a result of this method.

And I no longer had to resort to the hard-closing tactics Frank and the heavy hitters needed to try to rescue deals in the eleventh hour.

The Turnaround

My real understanding of applicants began when I started to discover the *limitations* of the resumes, applications, and data sheets I was using to collect and process information.

Like most search firms, my company provided me with a variety of data sheets and applications used to interview applicants. These forms, along with resumes, were excellent tools for gathering all sorts of useful information.

The problem was that most of the information I gathered was *irrelevant* to my needs in formulating accurate evaluations.

For example, the data regarding an applicant's supervisors, former employers, and references was primarily used as a tool for me to write job orders, or get referrals. It had little real value in helping me evaluate an applicant.

Other questions on my forms were equally irrelevant. I've never needed to know the make or model of an applicant's car, or what the company's reaction was the last time an applicant asked for a raise.

But this was the sort of junk I was collecting, until I started to use a different type of data sheet.

The "Real" Data Sheet

The truth is, any piece of information is *potentially* critical in understanding an applicant and his likelihood of being placed. Who knows, maybe there's a deal out there whose very survival hinges upon the make and model of an applicant's car!

But unless *specific* information is gathered and properly analyzed, you'll always be guessing as to which applicant you should work with, or whether a deal is likely to close.

By *supplementing* your standard forms with a series of questions I call the "real" data sheet, you can make significant improvements in your ability to control your valuable time.

Why? Because when you cut through all the smoke and mirrors surrounding applicant information, your degree of "applicant control" boils down to your understanding of three fundamentals: skills, values and commitment. Here's how:

First, take an inventory of *skills*. These are the quantifiable statistics regarding the applicant's education, work history, salary, residency, product knowledge, and so forth. Skills are the most obvious traits you use in order to evaluate an applicant.

To find out more about an applicant's skills, ask these questions:

- What are you currently doing in your work?

- What have you done in the past?

- What is your education?

- Who (or how many, or what types of people) do you supervise? To whom do you report?

- What does your company do?

- What is your current salary? Past salary? What would you like to earn?

- What have you done which has significantly affected your company, career, or work environment for the better?

Next, turn your attention to the candidate's *values*. These refer to the subjective beliefs and feelings that govern the applicant's motivations. After all, aren't a person's beliefs and feelings responsible for his choice of occupation, geographic preference, and financial needs?

Here are a few questions you can use to understand an applicant's values, or life priorities:

- List in order the three things most important to you in life.

- List in order the three things most important to you in a job.

- Describe in detail your ideal position.

- Have you interviewed recently with any company which satisfied these ideals? What was the result?

- What are your long term goals?

The more you understand the things that are important to a person, the more you'll be able to satisfy his employment priorities.

A True Test of Commitment

Finally, *commitment* is your way of determining the willingness of an applicant to make a job change, and work with you in a way in which you feel comfortable and productive. Here are some questions that test a candidate's level of commitment:

- Have you ever worked closely with a recruiter before? If so, what was the result?

- What are your expectations of our professional relationship?

- Do you feel comfortable having me represent you? If not, why?

- Are you available for interviews on short notice? How short?

- Describe in detail any interviews you've been to in the last year.

- Give me your commuting or relocation guidelines. How will this affect your family?

- If I find you a position that satisfies your employment criteria, would you be in a position to resign your job and start in two weeks?

- What if, after you give notice, your present company offers you more money to stay? What would you tell them?

- (If applicant lives locally) When can you come into my office? I'd like to meet you.

- Can I trust you to remain totally confidential regarding any future interviewing activity?

- Will you keep me informed of any changes in your job, or subsequent interviews?

- Can you think of anything that would prevent you from changing jobs at this time?

These questions are designed to *qualify* the applicant and help you develop a true understanding of his goals and motivations.

In addition, the real data sheet will allow you to discover *needs,* which can later be satisfied.

Matching the skills, values, and commitments of an applicant to the skills, values, and commitments of an employer will produce placements, because you're satisfying two sets of needs. It's that simple.

With a clear understanding of an applicant's *motivational* bottom line, you'll forever take the suspense out of closing deals!

And best of all, you'll stop wasting time with inappropriate job-seekers.

Cutting Through the Ambiguity

Now let's spend a moment to sharpen your discovery skills.

We've all heard these statements from our applicants a hundred times:

"I want more responsibility."

"I'd like a position with more challenge."

*"I've never been given the sort of
advancement I deserve."*

But exactly what are these people telling you?

For all you know, *responsibility* may mean landing the job of making the department's coffee every morning.

Challenge may mean planning the company picnic.

And *advancement* may mean becoming captain of the company bowling league!

The point is, you should never accept terms like responsibility, challenge, growth, advancement, opportunity, promotion, or visibility on face value. It's not that the applicant is insincere when he uses them; the terms are simply ambiguous by nature, and mean different things to different people.

Such terms remind me of the vague, trendy babble typical of the personal ads I used to see (and regretfully responded to) when I lived in southern California:

*Attractive, slim, intelligent, loving, youthful, athletic
single female seeking man with same qualities for
long walks on beach, romantic evenings and
committed relationship, possibly with children.*

I mean, this could pertain to anyone! (But in reality, nobody writing this type of personal ad ever remotely matches their own description.)

The point is, you should make it a habit to zero in on what people really mean by getting *evidence* from them. Try using these types of questions the next time an applicant tells you he's looking for more "responsibility":

- Exactly how would you *define* responsibility?

- What *changes* would occur in your job if only you were given more responsibility?

- How would you *know* if you suddenly had more responsibility?

- Describe to me the *function* of someone you know who currently has the responsibility you are seeking.

- If you were to get more responsibility, what would this *mean* to you?

- What *feelings* do you attach to greater responsibility?

- What tangible *qualities* do you attach to having greater responsibility? Money? Prestige? Respect? Power? Position?

Since no two people attach the same meaning to common terminology, it's important to eliminate the ambiguity from applicant responses.

Defining Applicant Categories

Do all applicants merit the same exhaustive questioning and analysis? Of course not; you simply don't have the time.

Therefore, you must place your applicants into one of three categories, according to your ability to help them.

Please remember, though, that all people are special in their own way, and our grading system in no way reflects upon their value as human beings. Never confuse your professional judgment with moral judgment, nor be unkind or disrespectful to those you cannot help.

- *Throw Away* applicants are those who have skills or motivations that are totally unrelated to your ability to help them. Unless you see yourself as a social worker, be kind and polite to these people, but don't waste your time with them.

- *File Away* applicants are those whose professional skills and motivations fall within the boundaries of your desk specialty. Spend enough time with them in order to get a reasonably good picture of what their strengths are, and what would motivate them to change jobs. Later on, you may find them perfect for a hot search assignment.

In the meantime, make absolutely sure to pick their brains for referrals to other applicants, industry information, and job order leads resulting from recent interviewing activity. These people will act as your "markers" for years, and will be very valuable to you. Other *file away* candidates include those whose skills fall outside your specialty area. They should be passed along quickly to other account executives who might be able to use them.

- *Right Away* applicants are the ones you spend the most time with. Use your real data sheet to carefully evaluate their skills, values and commitment.

Right Away applicants fall into two groups: [1] job order applicants; and [2] MPAs (or most placeable applicants).

38

Job order applicants are the bread and butter types who happen to match existing job orders, while MPAs are the unique applicants you can use to open doors and establish new accounts. Because of the special qualities of MPAs, we'll spend the next chapter discussing them.

A careful evaluation of every applicant is fundamental to your success. After all, we're judged by the company we keep!

The MPA:
Your Catalyst
for Success

*T*here's something special about the most placeable applicant.

To your prospective clients, the most placeable applicant (or MPA) is a potentially valuable employee whose special skills and personality represent benefits in the form of increased productivity, higher profits, innovative procedures, and a boost in morale.

Your MPA is also a very special person to you, since he represents the potential for placements, job orders, job order leads, applicant referrals, repeat business, credibility, and industry knowledge.

Your association with an MPA helps make *you* a very special person. After all, you are helping him to lead a more fulfilling life.

And your presentation of an MPA to a prospective client company not only gives them a golden opportunity to interview (and hire) a beneficial employee, it allows them the chance to see firsthand the quality of your work.

In effect, the MPA is your catalyst for success!

Defining the "Real" MPA

In a marketing campaign, the MPA represents your "calling card" to prospects. Since the right MPA will help open many doors, careful screening is extremely important.

We generally think of an MPA as a stereotypic applicant who satisfies a fixed set of criteria, such as having a specific background, or salary.

However, an applicant meeting all of the MPA criteria may prove to be unmarketable due to fluctuations in his industry.

Therefore, don't be surprised if the Harvard Ph.D. your clients were fighting over six months ago now has them yawning or rolling their eyes. Markets always run in cycles.

Be careful not to fall in love with a "blue chip" applicant who has no current worth to your prospects. Employers will always have the final say as to who's hot and who's not.

The same basic guidelines used to evaluate applicants according to their skills, values, and commitment can also be used to select a "real" MPA.

For example, here's a profile of suggested MPA skills:

•   Your MPA must have an education that's appropriate to your desk specialty market, and skills that are in demand.

- Your MPA should have an appearance which is presentable, and conforms to industry expectations.

- Your MPA should have the ability to communicate effectively.

- Your MPA must have a good track record, which can be verified by credible, professional references.

- In the professional arena, your MPA should currently be earning between $30,000 and $50,000 per year, since most positions are available in the low- to mid-point of the salary range in any organization.

And in addition, your MPA must have quantifiable, obvious achievements that can be clearly presented to your prospective employer.

Tracking MPA Values and Commitments

It's not necessary for you and your MPA to share the same beliefs, priorities, and goals. However, it *is* critical that you understand and feel comfortable with the values of your MPA and that they fall within the cultural mainstream of our society. (In other words, don't knowingly present serial killers, outspoken political extremists, or pathological liars to your prospects!)

Here are some other characteristics of the "ideal" MPA:

- MPAs should have realistic expectations regarding salary and position title. (Someone who wants to double his salary, or rise from draftsman to company president in one year is *not* an MPA.)

- Only present an MPA after having gained a complete understanding of his values, goals, ideal position, and recent interviews and/or offers. It's also vital that you can empathize, build rapport, and establish mutual trust with your MPA.

Finally, you should determine your MPA's level of commitment, in order to work with him quickly and confidentially. Consider these points:

- *Interviewing.* Your MPA must be willing to interview on short notice (preferably within two days and during working hours), and be able to start a new job in two weeks. He must also be able to give you a powerful explanation as to why he will absolutely decline a counteroffer from his current employer.

- *Candor.* Your MPA must be willing to engage in an honest, confidential discussion with you when you first begin working together, and keep you informed as to any other interviews or changes in his career that my occur subsequently.

- *Realism.* You must be aware of the impact a job change will have on his family (such as a longer commute or relocation); or anything that would prevent him from making a change at this time.

Only after a prospective MPA has satisfied your criteria with respect to skills, values and commitment should you proceed.

Special Cases: Exceptions to the Rule

Occasionally, you'll stumble across a job seeker blessed with a truly unique background, or surrounded by an unusual set of circumstances. With a small dose of creativity, these people can become terrific MPAs!

A few years ago, when I worked in Los Angeles, I took a call from Jeff, an entry level candidate.

It seems he had been recruited by a large aerospace company while in his senior year in college. They had offered him an engineering position, which they said would be waiting for him in L.A. as soon as he finished school.

After graduation, Jeff had packed his bags and moved all the way from New Hampshire to California. His first day on the job, the company told him they were sorry, but the defense budget was recently cut, and his position had been eliminated.

Could I help him find a job?

This may sound crazy, but somehow, I *knew* I could place this guy, so I asked him to come into my office for a chat.

Here was a twenty-one year old applicant with a degree in mechanical engineering and no work experience outside of college. Not much to work with, right?

Wrong.

The moment he walked into my office, I knew from his rugged good looks, impeccable attire, and self-assured demeanor that he was someone special. His warm greeting and firm handshake immediately broke the ice, and I motioned to him to have a seat.

"So, Jeff, where did you go to college?" I asked.

"An Ivy League school in New England called Dartmouth," Jeff replied.

"Do anything special there?"

"Well, I did play a couple years of varsity football."

"No kidding. What position?" I asked.

45

"Oh, quarterback," he said.

"That's nice," I said. "What can you tell me about school? Any particular interests?"

"Well, I did some work in the sports medicine lab, doing biomechanical research using student athletes as subjects," he told me. "In fact, my senior thesis was based on our findings. The aerospace company that brought me out here to L.A. wanted me to work on the space shuttle program, concentrating on ergonomics research. Do you think you can help me find a job?"

"I don't know," I lied. "Any other special interests you can tell me about?"

"Well, I didn't have much time for outside activities, other than the academic honor societies. You see, I was pretty busy working nights as a bartender to put myself through school," he said.

Okay, I had heard enough!

Biomechanical Magic

By this point, I knew that placing him with a company was only a matter of how quickly I could dial a telephone! In fact, I felt like pinning an invoice to his jacket and counting to ten! What employer wouldn't want a piece of gold like this?

I walked Jeff to the door and thanked him for coming in. Then I literally ran back to my desk and furiously began dialing; after all, it was Friday afternoon, and I didn't have much time.

First call: the UCLA mechanical engineering department. Did they know of any companies doing biomechanical research in the Los Angeles area?

Well, yes. There's a little company out in Canoga Park called Accident Research and Analysis.

Great. Give me the number.

Second call: Hi, who's your company president? Oh, he's the only full time employee aside from the receptionist? That's fine. Would you put me through, please? Thank you.

Hello, Mr. Employer, this is Bill Radin. You wouldn't believe who I just met...

Well, you can probably guess the rest of the story. The interview took place Saturday morning. By noon we had ourselves a deal, and Jeff started his new job the following Monday.

The moral of the story is: there's money to be made by working with special case MPAs.

The Power of Creativity

I used to work with another recruiter who would get two or three calls a day from entry level applicants. His response never varied. In a tone designed to let them know how much they were wasting his time, he told them, sorry, I can't help you if you don't have experience, call me back in a couple of years!

I hate to think of all the money he left sitting on the table from having this sort of attitude.

Don't misunderstand me. I'm a firm believer that "our stock in trade is the obvious," so don't try and build a career around the special case MPA.

But do yourself a favor and keep an open mind to situations that fall outside the "normal" category.

Savvy recruiters are those who recognize
the value of placeable applicants.

5

Harnessing the Power of Benefit Selling

*N*ow that you know the features of the most placeable applicant, all you have to do is pick up the phone and start making marketing calls, right?

Well, not exactly. There's one more important step. You first need to convert your MPA's most desirable features into *benefits*.

The process you're about to learn is so fundamental to successful selling, it deserves its own chapter.

Feature to benefit conversion is one of the most powerful aspects of our business, as it combines human psychology with selling technology. Your mastery of this process will put you head and shoulders above ordinary selling professionals, and will greatly enhance your persuasion capabilities.

Definitions and Distinctions

First of all, let's define the terms, according to Webster:

- *Feature* --- a prominent or conspicuous part or characteristic.

Power steering, power brakes, and chrome wheels are *features* of an automobile.

- *Benefit* --- anything that is advantageous or for the good of a person.

A feeling of comfort, safety, and style are some of the possible *benefits* of power steering, power brakes, and chrome wheels.

To put the terms into perspective, you can use the following generalization:

- A feature can be looked at fairly objectively.

- The perception of a benefit, though, is highly subjective.

When making a buying decision, each individual attaches a unique set of feelings to any given feature according to his perception of need. It's quite possible that a single feature can produce a wide range of emotional responses, depending on the observer.

Ownership of chrome wheels, for example, may induce a positive feeling of status, prestige, or self-esteem in Fred; while the same set of wheels may spark feelings of individuality or aesthetic appreciation in Bob.

To John, however, chrome wheels may symbolize decadence, greed, or vanity; and stir feelings of anger, or resentment.

Clearly, then, a single *feature* is capable of arousing an infinitely wide spectrum of perceptions, or potential *benefits*.

Savvy selling professionals know that a person will make a buying decision based on a product's perceived benefits, not for its features.

To illustrate, let's look at how a powerful group of selling professionals exploits the principle of benefit selling.

Features and Benefits on Madison Avenue

Advertisers are very clever at linking up their clients' products with perceived benefits. They make assumptions through extensive market research that the specific audience they are targeting will find the perceived benefits to be pleasurable, and therefore, desirable to own.

Often, a product will have no distinguishable features to convert to benefits. In such cases, advertisers must maximize the power of the *product-benefit association.*

Beer companies, for instance, spend millions of dollars each year to produce television commercials. On a superficial level, these ads promote the rather commonplace features of their product: clear, crisp taste that's less filling, cold filtered or genuine draft brewing, and so forth. Do consumers really care about (or purchase) beer for the way it's brewed?

Absolutely not! People buy the advertisers' products because of the pleasurable feelings the "hidden persuaders" of television images and sound link to the products. Advertisers get us to associate their brand of beer with images of sexy men and women, sports heroes, warm friendships, family relationships, and adorable, cuddly canines.

The implication is that you and I will have these feelings if only we were to run out and purchase their product. Beer companies cleverly (and subliminally) sell us the perceived *benefits* of buying and consuming their particular brand of alcoholic beverage.

It's ironic that you never actually *see* anyone drinking beer in television commercials -- those images were banned by the FCC years ago! Yet the advertising tactic of linking product to pleasure helps fuel a multibillion-dollar industry.

But does everyone link pleasure to drinking beer? Of course not; think for a minute about Mothers Against Drunk Driving (MADD). They probably cringe when they think of these ads. So beer companies specifically target their commercials to reach an audience which their market research has shown to be receptive (such as the people who watch sporting events on TV).

Many fascinating theories have been published regarding the psychology behind advertising. In fact, nothing much seems to have changed since Vance Packard's landmark book *The Hidden Persuaders* was first published in the 1950s.

Basically, this highly effective form of persuasion is created by the simple connection of products to perceived benefits.

Features and Benefits
in Executive Search

Recruiting and advertising are two very different endeavors, but the concept of features and benefits is still fundamental to both. The major difference is one of flexibility.

Unlike advertisers, we have the luxury of being able to *discover* the desired benefits (or needs) of our prospects and then tailor our service so as to *satisfy* those needs.

By asking pertinent, open-ended questions, we can continually monitor needs and work to satisfy them.

The one exception is the "opening line" of a marketing presentation, which bears some resemblance to advertising.

Like the advertisers, we must make an educated guess based on our "market research" as to which benefits would likely be desirable.

Then, depending on the feedback we get, we have the flexibility to adjust our approach.

MPA Feature and Benefit Conversion

People buy benefits, not features.

Therefore, we have to be very careful to *sell* benefits, not features.

Think about all the data you gathered from a recent MPA (most placeable applicant).

Since I don't know your MPA, let's work with a hypothetical applicant, Mary Bradley.

Mary is a regional sales manager for a copier company. She has a bachelor's degree in economics and an MBA. In her three years of selling copiers, she has been promoted from a district manager with a territory of one state to a regional manager, supervising five district sales managers in a ten-state region. She was promoted because she personally brought in an additional three million dollars in business in her first year, a 200% increase.

Get the idea? This little biography consists of which, features, or benefits?

Hopefully, you answered *features,* since all we did was describe some of the prominent and conspicuous characteristics of Mary Bradley's career.

Now we're going to convert those same features into *benefits* that would be particularly interesting to an imaginary employer, the national sales manager of a competing copier company. Since we've never met the employer and don't know what he's looking for in a candidate, we'll have to make an educated guess.

Wouldn't it be safe to assume that he'd like to increase sales of his product in order to capture a greater market share? That would mean continued growth of the company, and greater job security for everyone.

And wouldn't it be desirable to have another highly skilled manager on his staff who knew the product and could train others?

Of course. And having a well-educated and articulate person such as Mary represent the product will give the company a distinct advantage over the competition, especially when it comes to selling to high-profile, prestigious clients.

Finally, wouldn't Mary's continuing success in sales, training, management, and customer satisfaction favorably reflect on the national manager, and help him gain added recognition and promotional opportunities within his own company?

Bingo! What sales manager wouldn't want these sorts of benefits?

The Absolute Necessity of Satisfying Needs

The selling professional recognizes that no matter how much a prospect talks about features, what he is really interested in are the perceived benefits those features (or the product) will bring.

As recruiters, we must constantly probe to discover a prospect's true buying needs, and work to satisfy them. When it is impossible to know exactly what the needs are in advance, as in the opening line of a marketing call, we must make an educated guess.

To sum up, then,

High-billing recruiters
are those who sell benefits.

Now let's put the power of benefit selling to work, by creating effective presentations to market our service.

Developing Effective Marketing Strategies

*H*igh billing recruiters recognize that marketing is a necessary and perpetual activity in our business. In fact, the characteristic common to all superstar recruiters is their ability to effectively and *continually* market their service.

Marketing creates unlimited opportunities for you to discover and satisfy needs. If acted upon, these opportunities will translate into increased levels of meaningful activity, such as job orders, sendouts, recruiting calls, and placements. This activity, in turn, will lead to higher billings.

By far the most powerful marketing tool is your MPA.

As we learned in chapter five, the MPA is a potentially valuable employee whose special skills and personality represent increased productivity, higher profits, innovative procedures, and a boost in morale to your clients.

A well-conceived and executed MPA presentation to prospective employers will stimulate their interest, which will lead to the dialogue necessary for you to probe for, and ultimately satisfy, needs.

Marketing your MPA for maximum results is simply a matter of combining basic selling skills with a checklist of objectives.

Benefit Selling in Candidate Marketing

We've already learned that no matter how much a prospect talks about features, what he or she is really interested in are the perceived *benefits* those features will bring.

Therefore, an effective marketing call begins with a clear statement of the MPA's potential benefits to the employer, followed by a question which tests for acceptance, and creates dialogue.

Using Mary Bradley as a hypothetical MPA, compare the following presentations:

Recruiter: Mr. Employer, let me tell you about Mary Bradley.

Mary has a degree in economics, and an MBA. She's currently a regional manager with one of your competitors, supervising ten district managers, and she increased

58

sales in her territory by two hundred per cent her first year in the business.

Isn't this the sort of person you could use in your organization?

This presentation of *features* may produce results, but only because the candidate is so obviously talented. Now let's look at a marketing call that presents *benefits:*

Recruiter: Mr. Employer, if you heard about a way in which you could increase sales by two hundred percent, capture a greater market share, effectively train your staff, and consistently present your product to customers in a distinctive and articulate manner, wouldn't you be interested?"

Unquestionably, the presentation of *benefits* is a more powerful means of creating interest! Why is creating interest so important?

Because interest on the part of the prospect leads to *dialogue.*

Dialogue: The Inner Game of Tennis

Dialogue is particularly important in our business, for two reasons:

1] By its nature, our service consists of a complex and often lengthy series of transactions, in which a continual flow of information is essential. It is impossible to accurately discover and satisfy needs without dialogue.

2] Recruiting is largely dependent upon networking for referrals, marketing leads, recommendations and references. Your ability to initiate high quality dialogue directly affects the amount of information you receive.

Sometimes, a buying decision will be made despite the absence of dialogue.

But overwhelmingly, successful selling and recruiting can be directly linked to the quantity and quality of dialogue with your prospects.

Dialogue to selling is much like a good, long *volley* is to tennis.

As you know, in the sport of tennis, play begins once the ball is served. A sustained, interesting volley between skilled, evenly matched participants creates the most satisfaction to both players and spectators alike.

Failure to put the ball in play by "double faulting" the serve will end the game very quickly, giving neither the players nor the spectators much satisfaction.

A weak marketing presentation is similar to a double fault.

On the other hand, hard-closing the prospect has the same effect as service acing your tennis opponent. You may win the game, but he'll never want to play with you again!

An effective marketing presentation, then, should be of sufficient strength to create enough interest on the part of your prospect to make him want to volley with you.

And, naturally, your presentation should be "served" only to a qualified decision maker. Otherwise, you may find yourself volleying with the ball boy, the line judge, or a spectator in the third row!

Creating an Effective Marketing Presentation

To serve a strong opening line (or "grabber"), try to imagine the benefits which would be of most interest to your prospect, based on the MPA and your own market research.

Similar to advertising, your market research assumes that the people you call on will be receptive, since your MPA will be potentially beneficial to them. Your prospects will consist of a list of decision makers who work for companies who might employ someone like your MPA.

Your research may also uncover a particularly interesting situation at one of these companies. Perhaps you've learned, for example, that the prospect's company is opening a new facility, or expanding its staff, or bringing a new product to market, or acquiring a new computer system. Such information can be especially useful in tailoring your presentation.

To design your next marketing call, make the following preparations:

- Compile a list of prospects, making certain to identify potential needs the prospect may have;

- Carefully translate your MPA's features into a powerful series of benefits;

- Prepare (or script) a presentation of these benefits; and

- Follow your script with a question designed to test for acceptance and create dialogue, such as "How does she sound to you?" or "What are your thoughts?" or "How could you best utilize her skills?"

In order to put the ball in play, you need to present benefits to decision-making prospects in a thoughtfully constructed script. The greater the power of the benefits you present, the more likely your chance of scoring points with the prospect, or making a sale.

Marketing Call Objectives

Making a marketing call presentation without a specific set of objectives is like going to the grocery store without a list. If you're like me, you'll always manage to forget something.

Therefore, write out your objectives in advance, and check them off as you cover them.

There are six key objectives to every marketing call:

1] *Arrange a sendout,* provided you've qualified your prospect regarding his ability to make a hiring decision and pay a fee.

2] *Write a job order* to cover your MPA sendout. This will confirm your agreement with the employer regarding both the interview time and your terms and conditions. It will also uncover additional employer needs and provide information necessary to intelligently brief your MPA for the interview.

3] *Write an alternate job order.* Often, you will find that the prospective employer has other hiring needs in his department, or can lead you to other managers in the company who are staffing up or might be interested in your MPA.

4] *Get referrals* to people in other companies for whom your MPA's skills would be appropriate.

An appropriate referral script might sound something like this: "Mr. Employer, you're infinitely more knowledgeable about the industry that I am. Could you help me out by suggesting any other companies for which Mary's skills might be appropriate? Xerox? Terrific. Who do you know over there?"

5] *Probe for information* relating to the prospect's company. The more you know about the industry in general and the prospect's company in particular, the more you'll be able to satisfy their needs in the future.

Therefore, you might ask, "Mr. Employer, I've heard that your company will be expanding later this year. How will that growth affect your staffing needs?" Or, "Could you please tell me the most critical skill you'll need when your company begins its expansion?"

6] *Establish rapport* with the prospect in your discussion of topics relevant to the previous five objectives.

Let him know that you specialize in the placement of professionals like himself, and ask the question, "Are you the type of person that would like to stay abreast of opportunities in your industry?"

Decision makers are candidates, too. Why not explore their career needs?

Naturally, you need to be careful not to give conflicting signals. Your best business judgment probably would prohibit you from arranging a sendout and recruiting your decision maker simultaneously!

One of the benefits of high quality dialogue is that it tends to break down resistance. Therefore, be sure to recheck your list of objectives before terminating a marketing call. After an initial refusal, meaningful discussion may reveal, for example, that your MPA actually would be of great benefit to the employer. Don't give up, keep trying. Persistence will always pay off.

By consistently and aggressively pursuing all six marketing call objectives, every conversation with a qualified decision maker should produce results.

By establishing a benefits-oriented dialogue
with your prospects, you can satisfy all
six marketing call objectives.

7

Job Order Heaven: How to Write and Fill More Job Orders

*S*urprise! You just made the greatest MPA phone presentation of your life, and the decision maker couldn't care less.

But it seems there's this *very* important position the company has been *dying* to fill. Could you help them?

Doing your best to conceal excitement, you furiously scribble down every shred of information concerning the job, search status, and fee. Promising to get back to the employer the minute a qualified applicant turns up, you hang up the phone, throw down your pen, and literally float, job order in hand, into your manager's office to share the good news.

"Excellent!" he chortles, scanning your paperwork. "That's the sixth job order you've written this week."

You gloat.

"Keep this up and you'll have quite a quarter. Too bad about last quarter, though."

"Yeah." *Did he have to remind me?*

"Just keep writing those job orders, and something's bound to happen."

"Right. Talk to you later."

What's been happening to my desk, you think, as you close the manager's door behind you. *This month's been okay, but I hit a dry spell last quarter that almost killed me.*

Oh, well, why worry about it? I just wrote a hot new job order. And like they say: "Keep writing those job orders, and something's bound to happen."

Suddenly it strikes you. Job orders, *job orders*. Hmmm.

You have no problem *writing* them. You just have a problem *filling* them.

Let's check the status on some of those "hot" job orders you decided to work:

- *Job order number one:* You sent out twelve applicants to your client, and at the last minute an internal candidate was promoted into the position.

- *Job order number two:* You totally exhausted your supply of local applicants and were about to begin a national search, when the decision maker called to tell you that the position's been put on hold.

- *Job order number three:* You looked everywhere, and you still haven't found a single applicant interested in your client's position because the salary is too low. Sorry, the client says, the wage rate is set at the home office in Switzerland, and there's nothing he can do about it.

- *Job order number four:* The applicant your client showed interest in at yesterday's interview has just received another offer, and the client isn't returning your phone calls.

- *Job order number five:* You find out through the grapevine that the job order you thought was a waste of time has just been filled by another recruiter with one of *your* applicants!

Don't you *hate* it when that happens?

Secrets of the "Real" Job Order

Relax. Take a deep breath. Let it out slowly. Aahhh.
Now open your eyes. *It was only a bad dream!*
But honestly, doesn't *some* of this sound familiar? I mean, we have to write lots of job orders to stay in business, right?
And we have to try and fill as many as we can, right?
So how do we decide which ones to work?
Simple. *Just treat your job orders like applicants!*
Evaluating a job order is just like evaluating an applicant. That's because each job order can also be understood in terms of its skills, values, and commitment.
The following set of questions is designed to evaluate a search assignment, based on the criteria for a "real" job order.

- *Skills* are the technical requirements needed to perform the job duties. These might include education, prior experience, product familiarity,

67

industry knowledge, or a proficiency with systems, regulations, or languages.

Here are six questions you can ask the employer regarding an applicant's desired skills:

1] *What is the position title of the job you're trying to fill?*

2] *Please give me the salary range, plus any bonus, commission, car allowance, or other forms of compensation.*

3] *What are the responsibilities in terms of activities (in other words, describe a typical day), and what are the measurable, expected, results?*

4] *Is this a supervisory position? If so, how many and what types of people will be supervised?*

5] *To whom does this position report (name, title, background, length of service, and so forth)?*

6] *If the applicant does a good job in this position, what's the advancement potential?*

See how the questions correspond to the skill-based qualifying questions you should ask an applicant when evaluating his placement potential?

• *Values* refer to the subjective beliefs of the employer and his expectations of the applicant. Whenever an employer mentions an applicant's personality or his ability to "fit in," he is referring to *values*. Here are nine values-based issues to discuss with the employer:

1] *List the personal qualities you feel are important in a candidate.*

2] *List any professional or educational qualities you feel are important.*

3] *List any qualities, positive or negative, about your company.*

4] *Describe someone currently or previously in this type position. What do you like about that person?*

5] *How many people have you interviewed for this position?*

6] *Describe the best applicant you have interviewed so far.*

7] *Why did that person not join your company?*

8] *Tell me about your company's "vital signs" (product or service, age, number of employees, sales, employee benefits, and so forth).*

9] *Why should someone quit his job to join your company?*

Finally, it would be a good idea to ask for the names of the company's competitors and/or other sources of applicants.

- *Commitment* is your way of determining the employer's willingness to work with you in a way in which you feel comfortable and productive.

Common determinants of commitment are a sense of urgency, flexibility, responsiveness, and acceptance of our usual terms and conditions. To test for commitment, here are 16 questions to ask:

1] *Why is this position open?*

2] *What have you done to fill it?*

3] *How long have you been trying to fill it?*

4] *Exactly when would you like it filled, and when could you start a new person?*

5] *What would happen if you couldn't fill this job?*

6] *Describe your hiring procedure from start to finish. What about testing (drug, psychological, aptitude), delays, off-site decision makers, committees, or required signatures?*

7] *How many applicants have you interviewed for this position? When did you interview them? How did they come to you, through employee referrals, newspaper ads, or other search firms?*

8] *Are there currently any finalists for the position?*

9] *(If Yes) What is their status? Are you planning on making any of them job offers? When?*

10] *Has your company ever paid an agency fee before? How often, and for what type position?*

11] *The fee for my service is $_____ . Are you authorized to pay it?*

12] *(If no) Who else must approve it? Will you have that person sign my fee schedule and send it back to me?*

13] *Will you be available when I call to ask questions, present candidates, arrange interviews or get timely feedback? Great.*

14] *In case you need to reach me when I'm not at the office, my home telephone number (or pager number) is _____ . What's yours?*

15] *(Briefly) I want you to understand how I complete a search assignment. I work in three phases: recruit, offer and transition. Do you feel comfortable with this approach?*

16] *If I find a candidate who satisfies your criteria and wants the job, can you think of any reason why you couldn't hire that person and have him start Monday?*

Incidentally, it's helpful to *preframe* the employer before launching into an interrogation, so tell him exactly what you are about to do, in the following manner:

Recruiter: Mr. Employer, I'm going to take you through a series of questions that will help me learn more about your company, the position you want to fill, and whether my efforts will lead to a successful completion of this assignment. Can we set aside the time to do this right now?

Employer: Sure. Fire away.

Assuming the employer is ready, willing and able to freely communicate his needs, you're well on your way to filling the position and satisfying his company's needs.

Wild Geese and Holy Grails

In order to evaluate the information you just gathered, ask yourself whether the job order fits the following profile, in terms of expected skills.

- You are working with the decision maker.

- The employer has given you a set of realistic requirements regarding an applicant's previous background, skills, and expected results.

- The employer offers a salary range which is attractive and appropriate to the market supply and demand in his industry.

As to values,

- You have a clear understanding of the personal or educational qualities that are important to the employer.

- These values fall within the accepted cultural mainstream, and do not violate any personal or legal code of ethics, such as discrimination, or dishonesty.

- The employer has given you at least one good reason why someone should join his company.

- You have an understanding of the way the employer feels towards his company. (Do you want to spend your time championing a company with a disgruntled hiring manager? Think of the message this will give to your applicants!)

- You are aware of the type person this company has hired in the past, and their degree of success. (In other words, what kind of person does this company attract, and what sort of turnover rate do they have?)

And as far as commitment,

- The company is not in the final interview or offer stage with another candidate. (Why waste your time?)

- The company has a clear need to hire someone *now*. You have determined that the decision maker or department is experiencing some tangible degree of pain and suffering from not having the position filled.

- You are not in competition with too many sources simultaneously.

- You feel comfortable with the terms and conditions agreed upon, and you will obtain a signed fee schedule.

- The company is willing to work with you in a manner which you feel is comfortable and productive. (For example, if you prefer not to send resumes, is sending resumes a requirement for this assignment?)

- The employer will be available to you when you need him, and you have his home phone number, just in case.

- There is nothing currently preventing the company from hiring your candidate.

- The employer does not change the job description on a weekly basis, or after each interview.

And most importantly, you want to be sure that the employer isn't on a wild goose chase or a prolonged search for the holy grail. This would be evident from discovering that previous searches were unsuccessful, unreasonably lengthy, or involved an excessive amount of interviewing.

Job Order Categories

Depending on your evaluation, you may now place the search assignment into one of the following three categories:

1] *Right away* job orders are the ones you clear your desk for, and commit your time and energy to fill. These are "real" job orders, in which the employer has demonstrated his sense of urgency and willingness to form a partnership with you in successfully completing the search.

2] *File away* job orders are assignments that are currently unrealistic or for some reason unfillable. They are characterized by either a lack urgency or an absence of commitment on the part of the employer. Due to changing conditions, these may eventually be upgraded to *right away* job orders, so keep in touch with the employer to check their status.

74

3] *Throw away* job orders are rare, since you always want to keep your options open. However, employers who totally disregard the value of your service or have a history of deceit, nonpayment, or fee chiseling should be put on a "do not sell" list, with their job orders in the *throw away* pile!

Gathering Definitive Evidence

Like applicants, employers are also prone to using vague terminology.

Therefore, you'll need to dig deeply to clarify the true meaning behind terms which are so overused as to become meaningless.

Here are some favorite (but often ambiguous) ways in which employers tend to describe desirable applicants:

- *Applicant number one:* "Bright, personable, aggressive, dependable team player, with leadership qualities."

- *Applicant number two:* "Ambitious superstar, with the right chemistry, who can think on his feet."

- *Applicant number three:* "Presentable team player with a solid work ethic, who's good with customers."

Mostly, these terms refer to *values*. I have found that when two people have good "chemistry" between them, what it really means is that they share a common system of values or beliefs.

Be careful to get evidence from employers whenever you hear these sorts of terms by asking questions such as, "What exactly *is* a team player?" or, "How could you *tell* if a person

75

was dependable?" or, "What particular traits would *indicate* aggressive behavior?"

Not long ago, I was skimming the morning newspaper when I happened to notice the following classified ad in the "help wanted" section. I'll quote the first part of it verbatim:

PRODUCTION MANAGER

We want to hire an aggressive hands-on operations manager to take charge of our custom laminate contract furniture plant. We are becoming a major player in the industry and need a leader who can bring us experience from a larger and more diverse background to help solidify our position.

Do any of the terms in the ad (like *aggressive, hands-on, leader, diverse,* and so on) sound familiar? (No, I did *not* make this up!)

Drawing a Line in the Sand

Account executives are also guilty of an occasional stroll through the "land of the vague." Fortunately, the recruiter in this exchange was able to recover from his mistake:

Recruiter: Mr. Employer, I'm sure I can find you the right person. What sort of money would you pay for a superstar?

Employer: I told you already. Our salary range is $40,000 to $45,000.

Recruiter: I'm sorry, let me rephrase the question. You've just told me that the high point of your salary range is $45,000. Suppose I were to find a superb applicant who's interested in the job and has every qualification you're looking for --- but he needs $50,000 a year. *Should I not present him to you?*

Employer: Well, if he were that good, we'd better talk to him.

With a little bit of qualifying, you'd be surprised at the quality of the information you can gather, and how it will affect the outcome of your search activities.

The Work Ethic Issue

A few years ago, I had an experience that helped me learn the value of getting evidence from employers.

I was working on a search assignment for a new client, a giant, multinational oil company.

The company kept telling me that they wanted to hire someone with a strong "work ethic."

Shortly after my first sendout occurred, I called Mark, the hiring manager, to debrief him.

I could tell from his tone of voice that Mark was quite annoyed.

Yes, he said, the candidate had the right background, and yes, he could do the job all right. But the company would never hire someone like him.

He just didn't have the right *work ethic*.

"Wait a minute," I said. "The applicant attended a very tough college, and he's been promoted quickly at his current job, and he's got good references..."

"But didn't you interview him in person?" Mark interrupted.

"Well, no," I replied. "He lives pretty far from my office, and it just wasn't practical."

"Bill, from now on, I'm going to have to insist that you *personally* interview each and every applicant before you send him here, to see that he has the right work ethic," Mark said.

"You see, we'd *never* hire someone like him. He has a *beard!"*

This experience taught me that in job order heaven,

High billing recruiters always evaluate
and grade their job orders before investing
their valuable time.

Fig. 7.1 An article published in the trade magazine of your constituency will increase your job order activity.

Recruiting Strategies and Objectives

$\mathcal{A}$ single recruiting call can be more productive than any other form of activity.

That's because recruiting calls not only allow you to identify and establish rapport with people who are potentially placeable; they also uncover all sorts of valuable information.

In addition, recruit calls represent a form of *advertising*. They help spread your name and good reputation throughout your constituent industry.

Like a marketing call, a recruiting call can be carefully constructed to create interest, establish dialogue and satisfy objectives.

Recruiting Call Categories

There are three basic types of recruiting calls:

1] The *MPA recruiting call* is designed to develop a new MPA.

2] The *indirect recruiting call* is designed to identify third party applicants needed to fill a specific position.

3] The *direct recruiting call* is placed to a person you wish to recruit for a specific position you are trying to fill.

Naturally, your opening statement to each applicant will differ, depending on the call category. The basic *construction* of each call is the same, however. Your call should be designed to:

- Create enough conversational interest to "put the ball in play";

- Test for acceptance and stimulate dialogue; and

- Gather the information needed to satisfy all your recruiting call objectives.

Recruiting Call Objectives

Although there's practically no limit to what you can accomplish from an effective recruiting call, here's a basic list of objectives which you should always strive to satisfy:

- *Objective number one:* Gather as many names of applicants as you possibly can, and be sure to recruit the person you are speaking to.

- *Objective number two:* Gather data pertaining to the applicant's company and any changes going on.

- *Objective number three:* Get referrals to other companies and the people who work in them, such as applicants and decision makers.

- *Objective number four:* Find out where your applicant has interviewed, and get the names of the decision makers who interviewed him, in order to write job orders with those companies.

- *Objective number five:* If the applicant is a decision maker, see if he will give you a job order.

- *Objective number six:* Find out if your applicant will interview with your client company, and arrange the sendout.

By the way, do any of these call objectives sound familiar? They should, since recruiting call objectives are the same as marketing call objectives, in reverse order!

83

To illustrate, consider the following example of an *indirect* recruit call:

Applicant: Hello, this is Bob. May I help you?

Recruiter: Hi, Bob. This is Bill Radin calling from Santa Fe. Am I catching you at a good time?

Applicant: I guess this is as good as any.

Recruiter: Thanks, Bob, I'll try to be brief. I was told you might be able to help me with a project I'm working on. When the whole thing began, I knew it would be difficult, but I never suspected there would be so many nuances. May I explain my situation to you?

Applicant: Sure, go ahead.

Recruiter: All right. You see, I've worked for several years as a search consultant to the electrical engineering industry, specializing in power supply. My clients are all companies who design and manufacture medium range analog and digital components and systems, which are used in a variety of applications.

Just last week, one of my clients called to ask for my help. Because of their continued growth, they've decided to make a permanent addition to their design staff. They're very serious about who they hire, and as you might expect, they're extremely picky. They knew that because of my expertise and connections, I could find the perfect person. What they didn't know was how rare these people are.

Let me tell you, this has been one tough assignment!

Bob, I'd be very grateful if you could help me out. Who do you know that has a background in power supply design?

Applicant: Bill, I'd like to help you, but I'm not sure I know anyone who's looking to change jobs.

Recruiter: Well, to be honest, I'm at the stage now where it would be helpful just to talk with people familiar with the industry. It's not really important whether they're interested in changing jobs. Can you help me out?

Applicant: Hmmm, let me think. I've got a friend who used to work as a designer here named Ed Murphy. He's over at Babcock Industries now. You might call him.

Recruiter: Okay. Is there anyone else you can think of?

Applicant: Only some people here, but I'm not that impressed with their abilities, and wouldn't want to recommend them.

Recruiter: Still, it would be nice to talk with them, just to see who they might know.

Applicant: All right, why don't you talk to John, Frank, and Dave. But don't tell them I gave you their names.

Recruiter: That's fair enough. What is it about John, Frank, and Dave that leaves you cold?

Applicant: Well, don't repeat any of this, but they were hired before the new manager started working here, and they're just not familiar with some of the technology we're using, especially in some of the more recent projects.

Recruiter: What sort of technical knowledge are they lacking?

Applicant: So much of our work now is digital, and these guys are strictly analog.

Recruiter: So, it's frustrating, trying to work with people who can't pull their own weight.

Applicant: Exactly.

Recruiter: What's your manager done to solve the problem?

Applicant: The rumor is, he'd like to add another engineer to try and raise the overall technical level of the design group.

Recruiter: Hmmm. That would be an interesting approach. How do you feel about that?

Applicant: I have mixed feelings. I think I could solve a lot of the design problems, if only they'd let me.

Recruiter: Why won't they let you?

Applicant: I've only been here three and a half years, and they feel I don't have enough experience to do the job.

Recruiter: So they want to bring on someone new, and it makes you feel somewhat unappreciated.

Applicant: Right.

Recruiter: Bob, I know this sounds a little presumptuous, but I can't help asking whether you might be interested in a position which might be more satisfying than what you have right now. Would you be receptive to talking with me about it?

Applicant: Sure. As a matter of fact, I've been doing some interviewing in the local area.

Recruiter: No kidding. Who have you talked to?

Applicant: Well, I've been over to Silicon Designs and to Magnetek...

Recruiter: Sorry to interrupt, but was that Steve Schmidt you talked to at Magnetek? He's a good friend of mine.

Applicant: No, it was Jim Alexander.

Recruiter: What does he do there?

Applicant: He's the director of engineering.

Recruiter: How did you hear about that job?

Applicant: The recruiter that placed me in my present job set up the interview.

Recruiter: Bob, I really want to continue this conversation and learn more about you, so let's make sure we know how to reach each other. Give me your home phone number, and we can talk this evening. I know you must have work to do.

Applicant: You're right, I've got a meeting to go to in about three minutes. Here's my number. Can you call me around eight o'clock tonight?

Recruiter: Absolutely. I'm looking forward to it.

Applicant: Okay, I'll talk to you tonight. Bye.

Getting the Most out of Each Call

Clearly, much was accomplished in this five minute conversation, so let's examine it closely.

First of all, the recruiter created interest by asking for help and involvement. The recruiter also asked questions that tested for acceptance and stimulated high quality dialogue.

And most importantly, the recruiter was able to satisfy each of the six recruiting call objectives. Take a look at each objective, and how the recruiter got results by skillfully directing the flow of conversation:

Objective one: Gather as many names of applicants as you possibly can, and be sure to recruit the person you are speaking to.

Result: The recruiter was given the names of five potential applicants, Ed Murphy

	at Babcock, John, Frank, and Dave at the applicant's company, and Jim Alexander at Magnetek. In addition, Bob became an applicant, possibly an MPA.
Objective two:	Gather accurate data pertaining to the applicant's company and any changes going on.
Result:	We now know that a new manager in the applicant's company wants to hire another person because of technological changes in the product.
Objective three:	Get referrals to other companies and the people who work in them, such as applicants and decision makers.
Result:	We now know that Jim Alexander is the director of engineering at Magnetek, Ed Murphy is a designer at Babcock, and that EG&G also makes a similar product.
Objective four:	Find out where your applicant has interviewed, and get the names of the decision makers who interviewed him, in order to write job orders with those companies.
Result:	It's safe to assume that the recruiter's next call will be to Jim Alexander.
Objective five:	If the applicant is a decision maker, see if he will give you a job order.

Result: Unfortunately, Bob isn't a decision
                           maker, but we can easily get in touch
                           with the new manager who wants to
                           fill a design position.

Objective six: Find out if your applicant will
                           interview with your client company,
                           and arrange the sendout.

Result: That's exactly what we're going to
                           do tonight, when we interview Bob.

Was anything else accomplished? Yes, three things in particular:

1] We know that the applicant's company will pay a search fee.

2] We also know that Magnetek is working with a recruiter to fill its position; and

3] The recruiter was able to establish credibility and present his name, credentials and reputation to a well-connected person in the industry.

During the course of conversation, it's very easy to become distracted, and stray from the specific talking points that will inevitably lead to success. However, by establishing dialogue with recruited candidates,

High Billing recruiters consistently gather
the information needed to satisfy their
recruiting call objectives.

Fig. 8.1 Recruiting call objectives are essential to the success of your business --- as long as they're consistently satisfied.

Recruiting Call Objectives

• *Instructions:*   *Every time you make a recruiting call, try to satisfy the following objectives. Failure to do so may cost you money!*

1.   *RECRUIT.*
   Gather as many names of applicants as you possibly can, and be sure to recruit the person you are speaking to.

2.   *COMPANY INFORMATION.*
   Gather data pertaining to the applicant's company and any changes that may be going on.

3.   *INTERVIEWING HISTORY.*
   Get referrals to other companies and the people who work in them, such as applicants and decision makers.

4.   *REFERRAL COMPANIES.*
   Find out where your applicant has interviewed, and get the names of the decision makers who interviewed him, in order to write job orders with those companies.

5.   *SEARCH ASSIGNMENTS.*
   If the applicant is a decision maker, see if he or she will give you a job order.

6.   *SENDOUT.*
   Find out if your applicant will interview with your client company, and arrange the sendout.

The
Power of
Client-Centered
Selling

*S*elling involves the effective communication of information or ideas to others.

A *sale* occurs when the prospect accepts the information or ideas as being beneficial, thereby satisfying a need.

Like a language in which there are many dialects, selling has many dialects.

In this chapter, we'll examine different selling dialects in order to improve our basic selling skills, and to give you more flexibility in your approach to different situations and different types of prospects.

The Traditional Selling Dialect

In the selling process, prospects are often receptive to our ideas or new information.

Other times, we encounter resistance or concern.

In our profession, we commonly refer to these concerns as "objections." Traditional selling methods encourage us to try and "overcome" objections with "rebuttals."

Rebuttals are the responses a salesperson uses to influence the prospect's perception of need. Rebuttals are designed to:

- Cast the seller's point of view in a more positive light; or

- Weaken the point of view of the prospect.

Many companies in the recruiting and telemarketing businesses train their employees to memorize carefully scripted rebuttals to use whenever resistance is encountered.

Often, "flip charts" containing rebuttals to common objections are provided, in case the account executive's memory fails or he encounters an unusual objection.

The objection/rebuttal method of handling resistance or concern is merely one dialect in the selling language.

Communicating with your prospect in this dialect can be worthwhile, provided both of you feel comfortable and productive.

However, this methodology represents only one of several ways to skin the proverbial cat. As we'll see, alternatives exist that may produce a more favorable outcome, especially in today's consumer-sensitive climate.

A New Era in Selling

You've probably noticed a conspicuous absence of rebuttals and hard closes in *Billing Power!* That's because of the recent changes that have occurred in the selling profession.

In order to become more responsive to an increasingly sophisticated (and "sales resistant") society, the selling profession has had to shift its emphasis away from *overcoming objections* towards *satisfying needs.* Many contemporary selling experts have found that the old-style objection/rebuttal dialect has serious limitations as an effective selling technique.

This is especially true in our business, since we deal with issues that are far too important and complex to be trivialized or steamrollered by simplistic, insensitive rebuttals or hard-closing sales techniques. You and I have a responsibility to truly serve the best interests of our candidates and clients, and in order to do so, we must make a sincere effort to clearly understand their concerns.

Recruiting vs. Telemarketing

Although recruiters use the telephone as the principal instrument of making sales, it's important to remember that we're different than telemarketers in the following ways:

- *Unit price per sale.* Our fees are far greater than those of the dinner-interrupters who pitch long distance services and home water softeners.

- *Complexity of sale.* Completing a search assignment is like a Rubik's Cube when it comes to piecing together all the parts prior to a successful outcome.

- *Selling cycle*. Putting a deal together from the first marketing call to the start date of a candidate may take weeks, months or even years. In fact, I recently placed a candidate I had first approached nearly a decade earlier.

- *Relationship formation*. The marriage between a candidate and an employer is built on a bedrock of trust and rapport --- to a much greater degree (and with much higher stakes) than with a telemarketer whose goal is to put another VISA card in your wallet.

- *Repeat business*. Let's suppose a really skillful telemarketer caught you in a buying mood. Great. But how many times can you join the Sierra Club? By contrast, how many candidates can you place with a single client company over a period of years?

- *Syntax and level of professionalism*. To me, the most annoying aspect of a telemarketing call is the sales person's carelessness with the pronunciation of my name, and the lack of professional demeanor. A recruiter wouldn't last two weeks in the search business without the ability to express himself with at least a modicum of sophistication.

One of the enduring dilemmas facing the person who takes the sales profession seriously is that no prospect likes the feeling of being "hard closed" by a self-serving salesperson.

As in the game of tennis, you may "ace" your serve to win the match, but don't be surprised tomorrow if you find the other player volleying with someone new!

How, then, do we best serve the interests of our prospects in this new era, yet continue to make sales?

Client-Centered Selling

Nearly half a century ago, a prominent clinical psychologist named Carl Rogers (1902-1987) developed and perfected a method of counseling called *client-centered therapy*. He discovered that by using a "non-directive" approach with his patients (or "clients"), he could produce rapid, beneficial results.

By allowing the client to freely discuss his feelings and concerns in an atmosphere of unconditional acceptance, Rogers was able to break down the usual fear, inhibition, and resistance that clients commonly associated with therapy.

The client-centered approach was unique in that it made no presumptions about the client's feelings or concerns, or how they should be handled. The therapist simply acknowledged his understanding of what the client expressed, and served as a neutral "sounding board."

Later, it was discovered that the "client-centered" techniques used in Rogers' therapy could also be effectively applied to the fields of education, business management, and *selling*.

Client-centered selling is a selling philosophy and application of techniques based upon the work of Carl Rogers. It provides the selling professional with an alternative strategy to the traditional objection/rebuttal method of handling concerns.

In addition, the client-centered approach to selling helps break down "sales resistance" and allows both the seller and the prospect to discover *needs*.

Once a prospect's *needs* are discovered, it becomes a simple matter to *satisfy* them!

Later, we'll compare client-centered selling with the objection/rebuttal approach.

Fig. 9.1 Linking the appropriate feeling words to commonly felt emotions will help you build rapport and reduce sales tension.

Feeling Words

- *Instructions:* To express empathy, restate the candidate or employer's emotions or concerns with the appropriate adjective(s).

EMOTION	FEELING WORDS
Positive self-esteem	competent, confident, determined, proud, fulfilled, capable, needed, secure, important, appreciated
Negative self-esteem	embarrassed, ashamed, humiliated, guilty, insecure, ignored, neglected, unimportant, unsure, unappreciated, left out
Frustration	Trapped, blocked, smothered, burdened, overwhelmed, torn, frustrated, exasperated
Happiness	amused, happy, delighted, pleased, grateful, relieved, hopeful, elated, enthusiastic, glad, excited
Depression	lonely, depressed, lost, empty, discouraged, rejected, helpless, disappointed, crushed, drained, vulnerable, sad, beaten down, sad, bored, confused
Fear or anxiety	worried, scared, anxious, threatened, nervous, frightened, panicky
Anger	mad, angry, hostile, furious, bitter, irritated, resentful, jealous, spiteful, agitated, upset, offended, slighted, cheated, disgusted
Caring or loving	sympathetic, warm, compassionate, bonded

Empathy: The Key to Client-Centered Selling

One of the most powerful forms of human interaction is empathy.

We all have the need to be accepted and understood by others. Empathizing is a way of showing another person that you understand their feelings or point of view, without necessarily agreeing, or expressing any opinion.

In a verbal interaction with another person, empathy can be expressed three different ways: by *acknowledging*, *paraphrasing* and *active listening*.

- *Acknowledging* is the mildest form of empathy, in which you simply let the other person know that you heard what they said. Phrases like, "Uh huh," "Sure," or "Right," are common forms of acknowledging, and give the other person the green light to continue.

- *Paraphrasing* gives you the chance to communicate your understanding of what someone has said by restating it in your own words. This form of empathy allows the other person to correct you if you have somehow misunderstood them.

For example, if a candidate tells you the new job is too far from home, you might paraphrase by saying, "In other words, the new job is beyond your commuting range."

Be careful not to parrot back what someone says, as parroting is annoying and fails to show any understanding of what has been said.

- *Active listening* is the most powerful form of empathy, in that it summarizes the *feelings* and *emotions* of the other person. Like paraphrasing, it also gives the other person the chance to clarify your understanding of what's been said.

The key ingredient to any active listening statement is a "feeling" word, which acts as an emotional "sounding board."

Creating an Atmosphere of Communication

Let's suppose a candidate tells you that he doesn't enjoy working at his present job. You might empathize by saying, "You feel *unappreciated,* and therefore you want to leave."

The candidate then has the option of confirming or correcting your active listening (or "empathy") statement. In either case, you have worked toward understanding the way he feels without necessarily agreeing or editorializing.

Empathizing is not selling; it merely lays the groundwork for selling by letting the prospect know that his concerns are understood.

Demonstrating your understanding will help create an atmosphere of open communication, in which you can more easily probe for the prospect's *needs* and present the *benefits* that will satisfy them.

Putting Client-Centered Selling to Work

With a bit of practice, client-centered selling techniques can be incorporated into your selling vocabulary.

For example, the next time you encounter a concern, follow this five-part formula:

1] Listen to the prospect's concern without interrupting;

2] Make an "empathy" statement, using an active listening response;

3] Check your understanding by listening to the prospect's reaction; and

4] Make a benefit statement, followed by a question which tests for acceptance.

5] Now listen to your prospect's response.

Here are two examples of how you might use client-centered selling to handle concerns, using the five-part formula:

Example number one:

Applicant: I'm not sure I'm the right person for the job.

Recruiter: You're afraid you might not fit in with the other programmers.

Applicant: That's right. Everyone else in the department already has object-oriented programming experience.

Recruiter: They've assured me that your combination of skills is perfectly suited for the job. If you were under no time pressure to come up to speed, how would you feel about accepting the position?

Applicant: That would be fine.

Example number two:

Employer: I've already got a dozen different recruiters working on this assignment.

Recruiter: I see. So you're totally ecstatic with the results of their efforts.

Employer: Well, not exactly. They still haven't shown us any candidates we really like.

Recruiter: It sounds as though you'd be relieved to find someone who is just right for your company. If I were to present such a candidate, would you be receptive to interviewing him?

Employer: I don't see why not.

Do you see how client-centered selling works? Rather than argue with the prospect, or present a better argument, the goal is position you on the side of the prospect, and objectively observe how the prospect feels. Once you've agreed on the emotion underlying the decision, you can suggest alternatives that are non-threatening.

There's an old saying that's as true in recruiting as it is in parenting or psychotherapy: "Sometimes, it's better to be loved than to be right."

The Prudent Use of Empathizing

The question inevitably raised in training seminars is whether empathizing is always the best way to handle concerns.

The answer is: No, of course not.

It would be ridiculous to respond to simple, factual concerns by empathizing. Consider the following exchange:

Applicant: Tell me again the total compensation package your client is offering. It's not clear to me.

Recruiter: You're *upset* with what they've given you.

Applicant: No, you dumb schmuck, I *want* the job! Just tell me what the money is!

The point is, there's a time and a place for everything, including empathizing.

Choosing Your Selling Dialects

Let's compare the traditional objection/rebuttal method with the client-centered approach, in handling some common objections.

Remember, the client-centered approach does nothing to directly "answer" the objection; it merely sets the stage for further exploratory dialogue.

Example number one:

Applicant:　　　　　　　　I get calls from recruiters like you ten times a day.

Traditional response:　　Well, this call just might be different from the rest.

Client-centered response: It must be flattering to be in such demand.

Example number two:

Applicant: I've been to three interviews with your client. Why can't they make up their minds?

Traditional response: They want to be very careful to make the right decision.

Client-centered response: You're worried they may pass you up in order to hire someone else.

Example number three:

Employer: Search firms like yours charge way too much money.

Traditional response: I wouldn't say that. Our service can be very cost-effective.

Client-centered response: You're unclear as to the value of our service.

Example number four:

Employer: The job-seeker you're telling me about is way overqualified.

Traditional response: Well, maybe he could replace one of your more marginal employees.

Client-centered response: It would probably create a lot of uneasiness in your department to bring on someone with his ability.

Example number five:

Employer: Let me be very clear. Your firm will give my company a 12-month guarantee. During that time period, if your candidate doesn't work out for any reason, you will refund 100 percent of the fee we've paid you.

Traditional response: That's crazy! You can't expect me to guarantee something I can't control.

Client-centered response: You're afraid the staff would be demoralized if you were to lose a key individual.

There's no "right" or "wrong" way to handle objections. But by learning to become fluent in a variety of selling dialects, you'll increase your ability to satisfy needs.

Selling in the Long-Term

My experience as a recruiter, manager, and trainer has revealed that the objection/rebuttal method tends to put prospects on the defensive, fails to establish rapport, and does little to discover needs or create need awareness. This method is best used when you're seeking quick results, and aren't overly concerned about continuing a business relationship. Of course, if you feel your prospects respond favorably to this approach (as some invariably will), then by all means use it.

By contrast, client-centered selling tends to dissipate sales resistance, establish rapport, and encourage dialogue which is conducive to the discovery of needs. Because the prospect feels that you understand his concerns, client-centered selling helps build long-term and profitable business partnerships.

High billing recruiters know how to handle concerns; and by satisfying the needs of others, they make more placements.

10

Negotiating for Higher Fees

$\mathcal{T}$he expression, "everything is negotiable" was probably coined by a frustrated recruiter!

Each of us knows all too well the zeal with which our prospects and clients hammer on us to reduce our fees, modify our terms, and extend our guarantee.

In fact, I have *never* dealt with a single prospect or client who, at some time or another, didn't want to negotiate at least *one* of these points! It's just a reality of the business.

Therefore, shouldn't we try to develop effective negotiating skills?

Negotiating: A Way to Satisfy Needs

In most cases, the terms "negotiating" and "selling" are interchangeable.

The truth is, negotiating *is* selling, only with a heightened level of *needs* awareness.

The key to effective negotiating is discovering and satisfying needs; your needs, as well as those of the prospect.

Think about it: if you are not discovering or satisfying both sets of needs, you are either arguing, stealing, or surrendering!

Excellent negotiators reach agreements in which both parties feel satisfied. Since our business is dedicated to discovering and satisfying needs, it makes sense that we should strive to become excellent negotiators.

Your ability to effectively negotiate will result in two things: greater satisfaction on the part of the client; and greater billings and peace of mind for you.

Four Steps to a Successful Settlement

You can become an excellent negotiator by simply following the four steps leading to a successful settlement.

First, *measure* what the other side wants.

Before you begin negotiating, find out exactly what your prospect is asking for.

I know this sounds rather obvious, but you'd be surprised how many recruiters "give away the store" after hearing the prospect ask for a concession which is totally vague.

The plea, "Oh *come on, you can do better than that!*" often results in enormous and needless concessions. Finding out from the prospect *exactly* how much better you have to do must occur before any serious discussion can take place.

Second, *qualify* the negotiation.

If your prospect is not sincere (or in a position to buy), or has completely unrealistic expectations, you shouldn't be negotiating at all.

What good does it do to settle for a reduced fee with a prospective client in the first five minutes of taking a job order only to find out twenty minutes later that he won't be hiring for another six weeks and that he's currently interviewing five dozen applicants from the ads he's been running for three weeks?

Or, how do you handle a negotiation with a prospect who wants you to fill a $60,000 a year position for a flat fee of $2,000? You don't. Move on to another prospect, or let this one know in a polite way that he's brought a baseball bat to a soccer match.

Here's an interesting story: I recently received a $15,000 fee which was promptly paid in full. Three years earlier, when I made my very first marketing call to the same employer, he told me that he was only willing to pay a flat fee of one thousand dollars!

At that time, I simply let him know that I'd like to have his business, but we were so far apart that it didn't make sense to talk. He understood, I kept calling him, and finally, years later, we were able to reach an agreement, and put together a deal.

By the same token, you must be reasonably certain that your service will produce satisfactory results before you proceed in the negotiation.

If you honestly feel that you can't fill your prospect's position, why waste each other's time negotiating?

Third, *probe* for pertinent information.

After you know what your prospect is proposing, and he is qualified to negotiate with you, try and gather every bit of information you possibly can.

What has been his previous experience with search firms? With whom has he worked? How did they operate? What did they charge? Has he been happy with the results? Why is he now talking to you? What are his expectations? What special services are important? Is price an issue? Are terms an issue? Is time an issue? What hidden forces are at play? Ego? Pride? Fear? Prestige?

In other words, take a careful look at what the prospect's benefit needs are.

Very often, there exists a critical hidden agenda, which will often prove to be the pivotal point of a negotiation.

You never know what secrets may be lurking behind the scenes. A decision maker once confessed to me that the only reason he was negotiating with me was to help his personnel staff save face. Any concession, no matter how minor, he told me, would appear to be a "victory" for them. Did I help him out? Sure.

Time, Information and Power

Finally, *assess* the situation.

There are three basic underlying elements in every negotiation: *time, information* and the assumption of *power*. Your personal inventory of needs, in the context of these elements, will enable you to make an assessment of your situation, and probable outcome.

- *Time.* Ask yourself: What are the time considerations in this negotiation? Is anyone under the pressure of a deadline?

- *Information.* Ask yourself: Do I know enough about the situation and everyone's needs, or am I guessing?

And by the way, what does the other side know about *my* needs? Not too much, I hope.

- *Power*. Ask yourself: Do I have an accurate picture of the relative strength or control factors in the negotiation? Who can least afford to walk away?

Now you must probe for your *own* needs and agenda.

How much do you need this job order? What are your chances of filling it? What will you gain from making concessions? What will you lose? How much anger or disappointment will result from making concessions? Do you actually need to make any concessions? If you do make concessions, what will they be?

You're now ready to reach an agreement, but remember that you can always delay if you feel you have to. It's better to put off a bad or uncomfortable deal than agree to something you'll later regret.

By the way, it shows a lot of class to hold up your end of a deal, once you've negotiated an agreement. Nothing is more frustrating or disillusioning than an episode of bad faith negotiating. People may do it, but you should try and stick to the high road. You'll never be sorry for maintaining an elevated standard of ethics.

Negotiate From Strength

Nothing results in more loss of income than negotiating your fee from a position of real or *imagined* weakness. Remember, not only do you leave money on the table from your concessions, you tie up your valuable time by working on discounted assignments. Such time could be better spent on more lucrative, satisfying job orders.

To help make an accurate assessment of your negotiating strength, use this "true or false" inventory before reaching a settlement.

TIME: True or False?

- I am not experiencing the pressure from any deadline.

- I have other fillable search assignments to complete.

- I am not entering the search at the last minute.

- I have (or can find) qualified applicants who are available.

INFORMATION: True or False?

- This is a "real," or fillable job order.

- This is a client who really needs my service.

- This is a potential client who's *worthy* of my service.

- I know enough about the client, the position and the market situation to make an informed decision.

POWER: True or False?

- The service I provide is valuable to this or any other client.

- The service I provide is well worth the money I charge.

- The service I provide is unique and special.

- I can do a better job than anyone else.

- I can make an outstanding living by working only with those who value and appreciate my service.

- I can walk away from a lousy deal --- and still maintain my skills, professional dignity and earning potential.

The more times you respond "true," the better your chances of reaching a mutually satisfying settlement.

Not long ago, I conducted a seminar for experienced account executives. One gentleman stood up during the session and told the group that he felt we overcharged our clients for the service we provided; that any fee over 25 percent is a rip-off.

I couldn't believe my ears! I was surprised he could face himself in the mirror each morning, feeling he's cheating his customers. Later I found out he's a perennial low-billing recruiter. *That* didn't surprise me!

Percentage Reductions and Volume Discounts

Before you ever consider giving a discount, please beware of two things.

First of all, "percentage point" discounts in our business are often misleading. If your standard fee is 30 percent, how much of a discount is represented by lowering it to 25 percent?

Your prospect will insist that reducing your fee by five "percentage points" represents a five percent discount.

Actually, you are lowering your fee by one sixth, or nearly *seventeen* percent! On the placement of a $50,000 applicant, such a discount would represent a loss of $2,500. That's a lot of money!

Second, prospects often lure us into a concession with the "volume discount" bait.

We're going to have lots of positions for you to fill later on, they cry.

All I can say is, use your best judgment, but be careful. I never saw a single volume discount scheme that worked, for me, or anyone else.

On occasion, I've let myself fall prey to the "cheaper by the dozen" ploy of a large company. But I'll be darned if I've ever placed more than one applicant with a client that's begged me for a "volume discount."

I've learned my lesson --- *take one deal at a time!*

Dealing with Counterconcessions and Exclusivity

The best strategy when discussing the price of your service with prospects is to let them know the benefits they are receiving, in terms of accuracy, time savings, confidentiality, cost effectiveness, and so forth. By building *value,* you often satisfy the prospect's concerns, and dissipate his desire to get concessions.

In addition, your discovery of needs will play a vital role in reaching a settlement. Here are a couple of typical scenarios:

Situation: Your prospect asks for a fee reduction.

- *Discovery:* Because his company is small, cash flow is the chief concern, not price.

- *Solution:* He pays your full fee, but gets to spread the payments out over 60 days.

Situation: Your prospect tells you that other agencies discount their fees, and asks you to do the same.

- *Discovery:* None of the other agencies has ever placed a candidate with the prospect's company, because they lack the specialization in his industry.

- *Solution:* You clearly substantiate your successful track record as a specialist in the prospect's industry. He agrees to use your service at full fee on a "trial" basis, with any discussion of discounts delayed until after the first placement is made.

If you do decide to make a concession, be sure to get at least one concession in return, of *comparable value.*

For example, if you reduce your fee, a possible counterconcession might be prompt payment.

However, be extremely wary of "exclusivity," since it can't be enforced. I've made too many placements with companies who promised exclusivity to other recruiters to have any faith in that kind of arrangement.

If you decide to make a concession and ask for exclusivity in return, be prepared for the consequences.

How to Spot and Neutralize Gambits

Gambits are negotiating tactics used in order to gain advantage. The sooner you learn recognize them and neutralize their power, the more you'll be able to deal from a position of strength.

Let's look at three common gambits that are used on us all the time, especially in fee negotiations.

1] The *hot potato* gambit is used to dump someone else's problem on you.

"I'm sorry," the prospect tells you, "but other agencies work with us at 20 percent."
Wait a minute, you think. *That's their problem, not mine.*
"What a shame," you reply. "I was just going to tell you about someone from a direct competitor who could save you $100,000 a year by automating your communications system. Don't you think his contribution to your company might make up for a few extra dollars in fees?'

2] The *higher authority* gambit implicates a third party who somehow stands in the way of getting what you want.

"I hate to tell you this, Bill, but I can't agree to your 30 day guarantee. The personnel department insists on a six-month refundable guarantee," the controller tells you.
Certainly the personnel staff doesn't outrank the controller in these matters, you think to yourself.
"Well, why don't you just ask them to waive the extended guarantee for this position," you respond. "Certainly you have that authority, don't you?"

3] The *good guy/bad guy* gambit manufactures a real or imaginary "thug" to bludgeon down your position with respect to price.

"Gee, Bill, you should be glad you're not sitting across from my boss right now. He's a tough son of a gun and would tear your proposal to shreds. Why don't you and I just reach an agreement now, at 25 percent, and we can keep him out of this?"
I can't believe it! He's using the old good guy/bad guy routine on me!

116

"No, I think I'd kind of like to meet your boss," you reply cheerfully. "Maybe I could learn a few things from him about negotiating!"

Look for these negotiating gambits and their variations the next time you discuss your fee, terms and guarantee. Recognizing them will save you a lot of money.

And remember, too, that whatever gambit is used on you can always be turned around and used on the other person. *Touché!*

When it comes to negotiating, you're often in a stronger position than you realize.

Intensity of purpose and the commitment to excellent service will enhance your position of strength when negotiating.

11

Strategies
for
Closing More
Deals

*D*eal closing is simply the combination of thorough preparation, plus the ability to gather, process, and correctly respond to the flow of new information.

Preparing for a completed deal is a continual process, and begins with the proper selection and qualification of applicants and job orders.

Making placements has nothing to do with browbeating, backstabbing, bribery, or any other form of hard-closing, eleventh hour manipulation.

In fact, strong-arm closing tactics are unnecessary, ineffective, and in the long run, counterproductive. Their use usually indicates a lack of preparation and understanding of needs.

"Client-centered" closing, on the other hand, is productive, effective, and completely compatible with high quality, frequent deal making.

After all, a deal is just the logical conclusion to the aggressive, relentless discovery and satisfaction of needs!

As long as an applicant and an employer are in "synch" with their skills and values, and have made a commitment to work with you, deals will flow smoothly. The closing and preclosing techniques we'll discuss in this chapter will further enhance your ability to help people get what they want, not force them to accept what they don't. And the more you help people get what they want, the more deals you'll close.

The Mechanics of a Deal

I like to think of the deal making process as being like an ocean liner passing from the Atlantic Ocean to the Pacific Ocean through the Panama Canal.

Since the ship must traverse a land mass that's several hundred feet above sea level, the designers of the canal constructed a series of water-filled chambers (or "locks") to enable the vessel to make its crossing.

In order to move from one chamber to the next, the water on both sides of a set of steel doors separating the chambers must be raised or lowered.

When the water reaches the same level on both sides, the steel doors are opened, and the ship can pass safely to the next chamber.

And so it goes, throughout the length of the canal, until the ship reaches sea level once again.

Closing a deal is much like the ship's passage. Thorough preparation by a process called *preclosing* will enable you to easily and safely navigate your prospects through the placement process.

The failure to adequately prepare, on the other hand, will make the passage pretty arduous, much like trying to drag an ocean liner by a long rope over a fifty mile stretch of land!

Preclosing: Putting the "Lock" on Your Deals

No form of preparation is as important to a deal as preclosing.

Also called *trial closing*, preclosing acts to confirm your understanding of what the prospect (either the applicant or the employer) is telling you.

More importantly, preclosing establishes a *commitment* on the part of the prospect to take certain actions or make certain decisions.

Preclosing, in effect, allows your placement "ship" to pass easily and safely through a series of "locks" leading up to the final series of commitments, or the "close."

Many of the questions used in the "real" data sheet and the "real" MPA and "real" job order inventories are specifically designed as preclosing questions. Depending upon the answers you get, you'll know whether to proceed, change course, or jump ship!

Preclosing should occur during every stage of your activity with applicants and employers, and particularly in the early stages of your sales relationships.

Here are some typical *applicant* preclosing questions:

Recruiter: If I find you a position that satisfies your criteria, would you be in a position to resign your job and start in two weeks?

Recruiter: The last time we spoke, you told me that if I ever came across a position in Oklahoma City, you would pay your own travel expenses to interview there. Are you still ready to go?

Recruiter: You've told me that if my client offers you a salary of $42,500, I can accept the job on your behalf. Is that correct?

And here are some typical *employer* preclosing questions:

Recruiter: Yesterday, you said you'd want to interview anyone who had AS/400 programming experience. How soon can we set up an appointment?

Recruiter: When I started working on this assignment last week, you told me that you could make a decision twenty-four hours after the first interview. Has anything changed?

Recruiter: Now that you've selected Arthur as your number one candidate, is there anything standing in the way of bringing him on board next Monday?

The consistent use of trial closes not only reinforces the commitment of your prospects, it helps expose any misunderstandings or misgivings that might blow up in your face later.

Trial Closing Opportunities

Whenever you interview an applicant or write a job order, you should periodically send up a strategic trial balloon, not only to check your understanding of what's being said, but to test the waters for future commitments.

In addition to the precloses built in to your data sheets and job order forms, there are other critical times to take the prospect's temperature. These preclosing opportunities include:

- *Interview preparation*. Whenever you schedule an interview for an applicant, you should fast-forward to the next step in the process.

For example, you could ask, "Supposing all goes well at this interview, when would you be available for the next round with my client?" Or, "What would your response be if my client offers you a job on the spot?"

- *Reference checking*. Whenever you check a reference, you should always find out ahead of time what it is about the candidate that *most* concerns the employer, and bore right in on the person giving the reference for information about the concern.

Rather than sidestepping an area of concern (which rightfully appears to the employer as an avoidance tactic), the best approach is to lay the truth bare. By so doing, you'll earn the trust of your client, and diffuse the very obstacle that stands in the way of an offer.

For example, if the employer is concerned that the applicant under consideration is lacking in "people skills," then you should be certain to ask the reference about the applicant's ability to get along with others, how the applicant's verbal communications affected his performance, and so forth.

Normally, such concerns lack the potency to affect the deal, especially if they're exposed. Trying to mask them only makes the employer suspicious, and blows them out of proportion.

It's like having a date come over to your house, and you just cooked a fish dinner. The kitchen is going to smell like fish, no matter what you do, so it's better to greet your date at the door and ask to be excused for the odor, rather than frantically rush around the house ten minutes beforehand with a can of air freshener.

- *Debriefing.* A carefully scripted set of questions asked subsequent to an interview will reveal many things, such as how the applicant and the employer perceive each other, and how they view the job in question.

More importantly, the post-interview debriefing, will allow you to ask preclosing questions, provided there's interest on one side or the other.

For example, by asking each side to rate the other in relation to other applicants or employment opportunities, you can get a sense of where you're at with the client and the candidate, respectively.

And by tentatively scheduling the next round of interviews or getting offer and/or acceptance commitments, you can position yourself early on as the deal facilitator.

*Fig. 11.1 A debriefing log not only provides data about the job,
it also sets up a myriad of trial closing opportunities.*

Interview Debriefing Log
Part 1. Candidate Debriefing

Candidate's name _____ Date of interview _____

Employer _____ Position to be filled _____

• Instructions: Ask your candidate these questions following a sendout.

1. How did the interview go?

2. Tell me about the employer (personality, skills, management style, etc.). Did you meet with anyone else?

3. How was the job described?

4. Can you do the job as the employer described it? Do you want the job?

5. (If not interested) Who can you recommend as a suitable candidate for this position?

6. (If interested) Do you have any concerns, or do you need any additional information?

7. What sort of money would you need to accept this position if it were offered, and how soon can you start?

8. Other than the salary or any concerns you've mentioned so far, can you think of any reason why you couldn't quit your current job and start in two weeks?

9. Do you currently have any offers pending, or are you interviewing for any other positions?

10. (If looking at other jobs) How does this opportunity compare with others you are considering? How would you rank them, in order of preference?

11. How soon can I schedule the next interview?

Making Final Preparations

Remember when we talked about the obligation to our clients? We let them know that we would only extend *acceptable* offers.

Nothing is more nerve-racking than helplessly witnessing a deal unravel because of an applicant turndown.

Last minute turndowns are the result of poor preparation on the part of the recruiter, assuming the deal is a fundamentally sound one (meaning the applicant and the employer genuinely *want* to work together).

There are two main causes of turndowns:

1] The salary offer is too low; or

2] There exist other needs or concerns that have not been satisfied.

To avoid turndowns, specific techniques have been developed to preclose the applicant on these two issues.

The first technique is a "bottom line" script to determine the minimally acceptable salary requirements of the applicant. The second is what I call the "porcupine" close, designed to handle any of the applicant's last minute needs, or concerns.

Bottom Lines and Porcupines

The bottom line script was developed by a former manager of mine. It has not only saved many deals from last minute disaster, it has become an integral part of every placement I make.

126

As an account executive, you have a right to know the *precise* minimum starting salary required by an applicant, *before* your client puts together a formal offer.

That's because you have a responsibility to protect your client from generating an offer in good faith, only to have it rejected.

Your applicant must understand this. He must also be reassured that you will disclose his minimum requirement *only* if the salary the employer has in mind is too low to be accepted. If that's the case, you will supersede, and work with the employer to make the necessary adjustments.

You must also let your applicant know that whatever his requirements are, they are *his* business; that as a recruiter, you have no personal interest whatsoever in what he earns.

The following is the same script my manager taught me to use. It's so good, I've never needed to make a single change.

Recruiter: Well, Nigel, from what you've told me, the job is just right for you. Now all I need to know is how much it would take for you to accept the position with my client company, should they make you an offer.

Applicant: Bill, I've given it a lot of thought, and I've decided that I'm going to need $45,000 to start.

Recruiter: All right, so if they offer you $45,000, I can accept on your behalf, and you'll resign your current position and start Monday.

Applicant: Right.

Recruiter: Nigel, let me understand what you're saying. If I can't get you $45,000, but can only get you $42,000, I should tell them you're not interested.

Applicant: No, I'd have to think about it.

Recruiter: Nigel, I wish we had the luxury to let you think it over, but I'm obligated to my client only to extend an offer that will be accepted.

Applicant: Hey, whose side are you on?

Recruiter: My job is to put good people and good companies together, not keep them apart. What you earn is your business. I'll try to get you as much as I can, but I need to know what you'll accept, so no one's feelings will be hurt.

Applicant: Well, I guess I could live with $42,000.

Recruiter: So I can accept $42,000 on your behalf.

Applicant: Correct.

Recruiter: So if they can't offer you $42,000, but can only offer you $41,000, I should tell them you're not interested.

Applicant: Exactly. I would turn down an offer of $41,000.

Recruiter: All right. I'll work to get you the best deal I can, but just so we're clear, if they offer you $42,000, I can accept the offer on your behalf, and you'll start on Monday.

Applicant: Yes.

Recruiter: One last thing. Let's suppose that in good faith, the company, for whatever reason, can only offer you the $42,000 you said you'd accept. Are you going to be happy working for them?

Applicant: Well, I'd like to make as much as possible; you can understand that. But to answer your question, yes, I'd be happy with that.

Recruiter: Good. I'll call you as soon as I talk to my client.

Applicant: Thanks; I'll be looking forward to your call.

The first time I tried this script, I found myself in an awkward position. Jerry, the applicant, was earning $40,000 and refused to accept a penny under $47,000.

When I called the employer, he told me his company had decided to make Jerry an offer.

"Terrific," I said. "What were you planning on offering him?"

"Well, we think $45,000 would be fair," answered the employer.

I could agree with him. It *was* fair. But it was also unacceptable.

"Mr. Employer, I don't know how to tell you this exactly, but I spent almost an hour discussing this opportunity in great detail with Jerry," I said. "He really wants to work for your company, but he'll need at least $47,000 to accept employment.

"He's not bluffing, or playing hard to get; he's serious. I agree with you that $45,000 is a fair offer, but I've gone over the whole thing with him many times, and he's told me in no uncertain terms that he will not accept anything less than $47,000, no matter who presents it to him. I'm afraid that if you want Jerry to come to work for you, you'll have to come up with another two thousand dollars."

Then I shut up and waited.

And waited.

Finally, the employer said, "Well, if that's what it's going to take, I guess we don't have a choice. Call him up and extend the offer."

I nearly fainted. "That won't be necessary," I sighed. "He's given me permission to accept any offer of $47,000 or above on his behalf. I'll tell him the good news and have him call you right away.

"By the way, for my records, let me confirm all the information: Jerry's starting salary is $47,000. His title is Senior Design Engineer, and his first day will be Tuesday, October first. Congratulations, you've got yourself a good man."

What do you think would have happened if I hadn't found out Jerry's bottom line before I spoke with the employer? It would have been a *disaster*. I would have gleefully run to Jerry with an offer of $45,000 (which the employer and I both thought was fair), only to have Jerry turn it down!

Then where would we be? Everyone's feelings would have been hurt, and I'd be trying to haggle with both sides to reach an agreement.

I like the bottom line approach. It's much more predictable.

How to Squeeze a Porcupine

The porcupine close is so called, because in order to be successful with it, you must close on each point.

Applicants are notorious for wanting "one more thing" before deciding to accept an offer. Sometimes, they have just overlooked a point which is important to them. More often, they are cleverly trying to "squeeze" every possible concession out of an employer.

The porcupine close puts all the possible "points" out on the table before an offer is made, thereby clarifying the applicant's concerns and needs. It also reduces his natural temptation to "nibble" for last minute goodies.

Here's a conversation that illustrates how to use the porcupine close to get a final commitment from an applicant *before* the offer is made:

Recruiter: Bob, we've made a lot of progress in the last few days. From what you tell me, the position looks perfect for you; so perfect, in fact, that you've authorized me to accept any offer over $42,000. Do you have any other questions or concerns?

Applicant: One little thing. I've already booked a flight back to Utah for next June. My brother is getting married, and I need to take that week off.

Recruiter: All right, so before I accept this position for you, we have to make sure that you can take that trip. Anything else?

Applicant: I'm not completely clear on their medical benefits. Do you know anything about them?

Recruiter: I know they're fairly standard in the industry, and should be comparable to what you have now. Let me double-check on that, but should I go ahead and accept the job if they are?

Applicant: Sure, that would be fine. One more thing. My present company is paying for my tuition at night school. Do you think the new company can also do that for me?

Recruiter: I'm not sure. Are your studies at night school related to your work?

Applicant: Oh, absolutely. In fact, my night school class helped me get my ASQC certification.

Recruiter: Well, then, I'll see what I can do. If I can't get you the night school tuition, does that mean you won't accept their offer?

Applicant: No, but it would be a nice fringe benefit.

Recruiter: Okay. Anything else?

Applicant: No, that's it.

Recruiter: You're sure?

Applicant: Yes, positive.

Recruiter: Then let me summarize. I can accept the offer on your behalf if the company comes up with at least $42,000 in annual starting salary. In addition, you'll need a week off in June to attend your brother's wedding in Utah. I'll check on their medical benefits and make sure they're comparable to what you have now. I'll also see if I can get you tuition reimbursement for your night school studies which are directly related to your work, but that's optional, not mandatory.

If I can get you those things, you'll accept and start Monday, right?

Applicant: Right.

Recruiter: Did I leave anything out, or is there anything you'd like to add?

Applicant: No, I think we've covered all the bases.

See how the recruiter closed on each point, tested for acceptance, and continually asked for corrections and additions?

By carefully getting your applicant's salary bottom line and satisfying *in advance*, you can preclose the applicant and set up a successful deal.

Skillful qualifying, preclosing and closing
will reduce your anxiety and
increase your billings.

Fig. 11.2 Employer debriefing clarifies your understanding of the client's needs and solidifies your role as the deal maker.

Interview Debriefing Log
Part 2. Employer Debriefing

Employer _____ Position to be filled _____

Candidate's name _____ Date of interview _____

• Instructions: As soon as you have debriefed your candidate, ask the hiring manager the following questions.

1. What were your impressions of the candidate?

2. What were the candidate's strengths?

3. Do you have any questions or concerns?

4. How would this person fit into your organization?

5. How does this candidate compare with others you've interviewed? How would you rank the top four or five finalists, in order of desirability?

6. (If the employer is excited or eliciting buy signals) When shall I schedule the second interview? Will this be an offer interview? If not, when would you be prepared to make an offer?

7. (If the employer is lukewarm about the candidate) Shall I send this candidate to other companies?

8. Are there any changes in the position or the search status I should know about (such as new specs, internal promotions, last-minute candidates, or a hiring freeze)?

9. Tentatively, what salary would you be willing to offer the candidate?

10. What would you like from me at this point (additional candidates, references, degree verification, etc.)?

11. How am I doing so far? Are you pleased with the service I'm providing?

12

Preventing and Diffusing Counteroffers

$\mathcal{N}$othing in our business has a more devastating effect than accepted counteroffers.

Counteroffers can destroy our morale, our faith in applicants, and the trust we've worked so hard to build with our clients.

In addition, counteroffers are costly, in terms of time and money.

As a rookie recruiter, I blundered into several counteroffer situations that could have been avoided. The precise scenarios were each different; in one case, the candidate changed his mind before he was supposed to start his new job. In another case, the candidate never showed up for work on his start date; and in a third, the candidate worked for a week at my client company, then succumbed to a delayed counteroffer and went back to his old employer --- with an enhanced title and a greatly increased paycheck.

Looking for Clues

Beyond having a bad gut feeling with respect to a candidate's true intentions, the signs of an accepted counteroffer are usually visible when you first interview a candidate. These signs are imbedded in the way a candidate responds to value and commitment issues, and include:

• Extreme indecision about career issues;

• Ambivalence about the candidate's current employer or professional peers;

• Exaggerated emphasis placed on salary needs or benefits;

• Creative obstacles placed in the way of interviewing or decision making;

• False claims surrounding professional achievements or narcissistic attitudes about workplace relationships;

• Unrealistic start date commitments; or

• Revelations or confessions about past counteroffer attempts or acceptance.

In addition to these early warning signals, you should also be aware of post-acceptance symptoms of counteroffer maneuvering on the part of the candidate or pressure put on the candidate by a current employer. These include:

- Sudden or unexpected commitments to the old employer, such as last-minute projects

- Secret meetings with supervisors or officers of the old company;

- Misplaced concerns (or demands) over benefits at the new company;

- Problems facing the candidate's spouse or children that were never mentioned before;

- Unexpected hardship surrounding relocation (such as the housing market, moving expenses, taxes, school districting, and so forth).

These preludes to a counteroffer should be viewed with extreme caution; and they may signal that a counteroffer negotiation is already under way. If such is the case, you know that your deal's extreme risk.

The Power of Selection

The truth is that accepted counteroffers are easy to prevent, if only we remember to use our power of selection, and the technique of preframing.

We already know that an applicant can be evaluated according to his skills, system of values, and commitment to making a job change, should the right opportunity present itself.

Obviously, an applicant's tendency to accept a counteroffer will greatly influence our evaluation.

To *test* for this tendency, we ask probing questions to discover the applicant's real needs.

If we discover from our probing that these needs are being satisfied at his current job, we are probably wasting our time with a "lookie-loo," an applicant who lacks the real motivation to make a change.

Another way to test for the tendency to accept a counteroffer is to confront the applicant directly.

Many account executives, however, make the mistake of asking the question, "Would you accept a counteroffer?"

Although that's a fair question, it puts the applicant on the defensive, and doesn't give the applicant the opportunity to *internalize* a counteroffer situation.

A more effective way of exploring the applicant's tendency to accept a counteroffer is to create a hypothetical scenario in which the applicant has to make a decision, as in the following exchange:

Recruiter: Well, Susan, I think I have a pretty good understanding of what you're looking for, so let me summarize. If I can find you a position as a hospital administrator with a small, private facility that's within ten miles of your home, you would interview for that position on a day's notice.

Applicant: Correct.

Recruiter: And if all goes well, and my client makes you an offer within the salary range we discussed, you'd be in a position to resign from your current job and start in two weeks.

Applicant: That's right.

Recruiter: Susan, I'd like to ask you something. Let's suppose the new hospital makes you a fair offer; and in good faith you accept that offer, and turn in your resignation.

What would happen if the people you currently work for were to offer you more money to stay? What would you tell them?

Applicant: I'm not sure. I guess it would depend on how much they offer me.

Recruiter: So in other words, you'd have to seriously consider staying where you are.

Applicant: Well, yes. They've been pretty good to me here. I just haven't gotten a raise in two years.

Recruiter: In essence, it boils down to money.

Applicant: Right. I'd just have to see who can give me the best offer.

Many account executives in this situation would either try to warn the applicant of the hazards of accepting a counteroffer, or would send the applicant on an interview, praying that the applicant might fall madly in love with the client company.

I would take a much different approach. I would scrawl the word COUNTEROFFER in big red letters across my data sheet, and put this applicant out of my mind.

Sending a counteroffer-prone applicant to an interview is like dating someone who is married. The odds of the other person "seeing the light" are so slim, and the potential for pain so great, it's not worth the trouble.

If you get signals from your applicant that he might take a counteroffer (or has taken one in the past), avoid him at all costs. Don't wear blinders or pray for miracles; find someone else to work with. The world is full of other applicants.

Preframing the Counteroffer Attempt

Preframing is a powerful technique that can be used to prepare a person for a predictable series of events. (Remember how we used it in Chapter Two to explain the three phase concept to an employer?)

Preframing allows an applicant to express questions or concerns which can be handled in *advance,* eliminating potential problems or misunderstandings which may occur later.

For example, if your client company is located in an old, run down section of town, you should tell your applicant before his interview, so he'll know what to expect.

Or, if the decision maker plans to be out of the country for two weeks following the first interview, you can minimize your applicant's feelings of impatience by letting him know ahead of time.

Preframing is also an effective way to *diffuse* a counteroffer attempt made by the applicant's old company. Preparing the applicant for a predictable series of events will take the surprise and flattery out of the counteroffer, and enable the applicant to see the counteroffer for what it really is.

Notice how the recruiter effectively preframes his applicant for a possible counteroffer in the following exchange:

Recruiter: Jim, my client is very pleased that you've accepted his offer. How do you feel, now that you're about to join a new company?

Applicant: Terrific! I can't wait to get started.

Recruiter: That's good. How do you feel about resigning from your current company?

Applicant: Well, to tell you truth, I'm not looking forward to it, but I guess I'll have to deal with it.

Recruiter: Maybe I can make it easier for you by telling you what to expect.

Applicant: That would be nice.

Recruiter: I've found that companies always follow a predictable three-part pattern when an employee resigns. Here's how it goes:

First, they'll be in *shock.* "You sure picked a fine time to leave! Who's going to finish the project?" they'll ask.

Second, they'll start to *probe.* "Who's the new company? What sort of position did you accept? What are they paying you?"

Finally, they'll make you an *offer* to try and keep you from leaving. "You know that raise we were talking about a few months back? We were just getting it processed yesterday," they'll say.

You see, Jim, we all act in our own best interest. Your company doesn't want to lose you, because it means they'll have to spend time and money to find your replacement. And that can be a real pain.

But the truth is, they *can* live without you. I'm just telling you this so you won't be surprised when they lay a guilt trip on you or try to flatter you by offering you more money to stay. They're working in their *own* best interest, not yours.

Do you think you're better prepared to face them now?

Applicant: Absolutely. I'll remember what you told me.

Recruiter: Great. And don't forget to call me after you've resigned to let me know how it went.

More than once, applicants have called me after they've resigned, to tell me that the old company followed the three-part pattern exactly as I described it. Not only were they prepared for a counteroffer attempt, they found the whole sequence to be almost comical in its predictability.

High billing recruiters qualify their
applicants and preframe them to diffuse
counteroffer attempts.

Fig. 12.1 Acceptance agreements and other last-ditch efforts to gain control of a candidate are rarely successful.

Acceptance Agreement

Entered into between (candidate)
and (search firm)

I, (applicant), agree to commence work for (client company) on or before (date). I agree to accept an annual starting salary of ($).

I understand that (company) is assuming the fee of ($). Should I fail to report for work, except because of extreme circumstances, I will pay (search firm) twenty-five percent of the fee in full within ten days from the starting date. That amount is ($).

I understand that there is no further liability to (search firm).

_____

Applicant signature

_____

Accepting for (search firm)

_____

Date and location

13

Advanced Strategies for Higher Billings

*I*f you're like me, you probably came to a startling realization soon after getting into this business.

You are self-employed!

Even if you work in an office with other recruiters, your desk is run like a mini-business, with you performing virtually every job function required to successfully maintain and improve the company's performance.

When you think about it, you're the company president, chief financial officer, director of sales and marketing, public relations manager, production foreman, and quality assurance supervisor.

You are also in charge of all the research, development, and document control; not to mention customer service, security, and human resources.

No wonder you're paid so well!

So far, we've concentrated on improving your fundamental recruiting skills and generic selling abilities. These are important issues of *quality*.

Now let's focus on adjusting the way in which you operate your business, in order to increase *production*.

By making the strategic and attitudinal changes in the next few chapters, you can work to improve your *profitability*.

The Power of the EIO

High billing recruiters use a program called the Employer In Office (or "EIO") to more effectively serve the needs of their clients, and thereby increase their own billings. (You may have a different term for it -- in parts of Ohio, for example, they call it a "trip in" -- but the idea is the same.)

Here's how the EIO works. At the time a job order is written, the account executive makes a quick analysis as to the quality of the assignment. If he feels he's working with a "real" job order, he presents the EIO program to the employer, in an *assumptive* manner:

Recruiter: Mr. Employer, I feel I can find the person you need. I will drop everything I'm doing and work nonstop on this assignment.

I'm going to reserve an interviewing room right here in my office for next Thursday.

I'll have four prescreened, qualified candidates for you to interview. Each of them will be capable of doing the job. You'll be selecting the one or two with whom you feel the most comfortable, from the standpoint of personal chemistry. The finalists you choose can then be brought back to your office in a few days for more in-depth interviewing.

The interviewing in my office will only take a couple of hours, since these are screening interviews, lasting approximately thirty minutes per candidate. I'm certain that out of the four people you meet, you'll want to hire one.

How does Thursday, around four o'clock, sound to you?

Before we discuss the fairly obvious advantages to you, the recruiter, think of how this program might truly benefit the *employer:*

- He knows that by Thursday, you'll have assembled a group of prescreened and qualified candidates for him to interview;

- He knows that his needs are quickly being served;

- The employer can maintain confidentiality in the event the position is being created to replace a poor-performing incumbent;

- He can eliminate or reduce the inter-office gossip that inevitably surrounds the trooping in of various interviewees;

- He can exercise efficient time management by interviewing four candidates in a single two-hour period;

- He will be free of distractions, since his mind will be focused on interviewing, away from the interruptions in his office; and

- He can make instant comparisons, and not have to rely on his recollection of candidates he met over a period of several days or even weeks.

Clearly, the EIO methodology is highly beneficial to any organization whose staffing requirements demand quick and efficient results.

A Feather in Your Cap

Now that we've established some of the employer-related advantages of the EIO, what are the benefits to *you?*

- You have received a greater level of commitment from the decision maker;

- You can debrief applicants coming out of each interview in order to better prepare the next;

- You can include applicants who may be slightly underqualified or overqualified for your decision maker to interview;

- You can use the deadline to put pressure on yourself to perform; and

- Job orders that utilize an EIO statistically have a much higher rate of closure than non-EIO job orders.

Although an EIO is designed for local assignments, employers will often make special interviewing trips from out of town in order to attend.

EIOs are an incredibly powerful tool, because they qualify the decision maker, establish control, and enable you to present a wider choice of applicants.

Expanding the Range

One morning, just as I was preparing to leave home for an EIO, an applicant called me whom I had been trying to reach for days.

Paul was a really nice guy that I met a year earlier at another EIO, and he had made a favorable impression on me. He was obviously overqualified to participate in today's EIO; I had just called to see if he knew anyone who might be a possible candidate. I began to describe the position.

"I'd be interested in the job," he interrupted.

"Paul, I'm sorry, but the top of the salary range is ten thousand dollars less than you're making right now," I told him.

"Isn't there any way I could talk to them?" he asked. "It sounds exactly like the kind of company I've always wanted to work for."

What am I thinking?

"Well, I'll tell you what, Paul," I said. "Why don't you meet me at my office, and I'll see if I can sneak you in after the last interview. I can't make any promises, but you sound so enthusiastic, I don't see that there'd be any harm."

Later, at my office, after all the other applicants had interviewed, I approached the employer.

"Mr. Employer, I have a favor to ask you. There's a candidate that I've known for a while that I talked to this morning.

"I had originally called him to see if he could refer me to someone for your position, due to his extensive knowledge in your industry.

"He's obviously overqualified for your position, but he was so interested in talking with you, and so sincere, that I told him to come down to the office.

"I don't expect you to meet with him, but if you like, he's out in the lobby now, and I can ask him to come in. What do you say?"

Of course, you know the ending to this story. The employer was so impressed with Paul that the company upgraded their position to accommodate him. A perfect example of how an EIO can expand the range of acceptable candidates.

The EIHO: Variations on a Theme

A variation on the EIO is what I call the "EIHO," or Employer In His Office.

On certain occasions, it's simply not possible for the employer to interview in your office. When that's the case, just gather up your applicants and hold the EIO at *his* office!

I once scheduled an EIHO with Dan, an employer whose office was in downtown Los Angeles. After the last interview had taken place, I met with Dan. He told me he had an interest in the applicant he had just finished interviewing.

"Hold on," I said, getting up from my chair. "Let me run down the hall and see if I can catch him before he leaves the building."

After flagging down the applicant, I pulled him into an empty office and asked him how he felt about the position.

"I like it just fine," he said.

I asked him if he had any concerns, and what sort of money it would take to get him on board, and whether he could start on Monday.

"This looks like a great opportunity," he said, "and there's nothing standing in the way. I could start on Monday, provided the company can offer me $29,000 to start."

"So if the employer made you a $29,000 offer right now, you could accept, and start Monday?"

"Right," he said.

"Okay, wait here," I said. "I'll be right back."

I dashed back down the hall to Dan's office and continued to debrief him. It seems my applicant was just the sort of person he'd been looking for.

"Well, it sounds as though you'd like to hire him," I said. "What were you planning to offer?"

"I think $35,000 would be fair, Bill. What do you think?"

"I think he would *probably* accept that," I answered, trying to keep a straight face. "Follow me."

Dan and I walked down the hall, and opened the door to the room where the applicant was waiting.

"Mr. Applicant," I said, "Dan has something he wants to tell you."

I watched proudly as Dan extended the offer of $35,000 and the surprised applicant accepted, agreeing to start the following Monday.

This deal may have come together without an EIHO, but it certainly wouldn't have happened so quickly, or been nearly as satisfying.

If you're not holding EIOs two or three times a quarter, you should start.

One recruiter that works for a company in California arranges an average of four EIOs a *month*. Of course, she also bills over $400,000 a year. See any connection there?

Winning the Game of Resume Roulette

Once there was a recruiter who did most of his work with personnel, discounted his fee, and sent resumes.

He made placements. A few.

He did this for about a year. Then he decided to change his approach.

He began to work only with decision makers, never discounted his fee, and never sent resumes. *Ever.*

And he made placements. Lots of placements. So many placements, in fact, that he more than doubled his personal income from the year before, and doubled it again the next year.

It shouldn't surprise you, then, to know how I feel about working with the personnel staff, discounting fees, or sending resumes; because that recruiter was me.

I've found that as a general rule, low billing account executives send resumes to clients for applicant screening, while high billing account executives don't.

There are exceptions of course. If you work a non-local desk, it would be unrealistic to ask an employer in Boston to buy a round trip plane ticket for a candidate in Vancouver, especially if he's never talked to the candidate on the phone or seen his resume.

In a local market, if you feel the need to send a resume, it usually means you've done a poor job of selling, unless your company's method of operation is *intentionally designed* to generate and send resumes.

Here are five reasons not to send resumes:

1] Resumes are inaccurate and often misleading. Your responsibility is to match *applicants* to jobs, not *resumes* to jobs.

2] Once a prospect makes a "no" decision based on reading a resume, that decision is almost impossible to overturn. The two of you end up debating over a piece of paper.

3] Sending a resume does nothing to establish your credibility or expertise. Once you send a resume, your role has been reduced to that of an impotent vendor, or supplier.

4] Resumes end up being passed around. Your applicant is no longer a well kept secret, he's now on public display.

5] When an employer demands to see a resume, he often means, "Go away, I really don't want to work with you."

If that's the case, why spend your time with a hostile or unqualified prospect?

Getting Beat to the Punch

One of the main reasons I changed my tactics regarding resumes was because of an incident that occurred early in my career.

I was working with a personnel manager, trying to fill a quality assurance position.

I had located and recruited an excellent candidate, and, as I had done in the past, mailed his resume to the company (this was before the use of the fax machine became widespread).

Two days later, I called the personnel manager to get his reaction to the resume I sent.

"Well, what do you think?" I asked.

"He looks good," said the personnel manager. "But there's a problem."

"Oh? What's that?" I couldn't imagine any problem; my candidate was *perfect* for the job.

"We've already interviewed him, and we're going to make him an offer," replied the personnel manager. "Sorry."

"But how could that be?" I cried. "Two days ago, he wasn't even on the job market. How did you get his resume so quickly?"

"We didn't. Some recruiter called the hiring manager yesterday and set up an interview without ever sending a resume. This morning the candidate came in, and we all fell in love with him."

Boy, did I feel sick getting beat like that, and losing out on a hefty fee.

Ruffling the Feathers that Feed You

Fortunately, I learned something from the experience, and was able to recoup my losses a couple of years later.

I was working with a new client in Detroit who asked me to find him an applications engineer.

It was a tough assignment, but I was able to fill the position in about three weeks.

A few days after the offer had been made and accepted, I received a call from the employer.

"It seems we've ruffled a few feathers down in personnel," he told me.

"Why?" I asked. "Is there something wrong?"

"No, they're just upset because the applicant you placed with me sent his resume to their department a couple of months ago."

"Well, that's not too unusual," I said. "Sometimes personnel gets so much paperwork, they can't keep up with it."

"That's not what they're upset about," the employer replied. "They're upset because they called him in to interview, spent an hour with him, and decided to send him away, because he didn't have the qualifications for the job."

"And now they have to write you a check for $13, 860!"

EIHO to the Rescue

This final story really sums up the point I'm trying to make about resumes:

I conducted an EIHO at the corporate headquarters of a major medical equipment manufacturer.

After all the candidates had interviewed, I sat down with the decision maker, and began to debrief him.

He couldn't stop raving about Barry, who had just interviewed for a position as a manufacturing engineer.

I was fully aware that Barry had never held a position as a manufacturing engineer. Yet his unique background and personality (skills and values, remember?) were perfectly matched to the company's needs, so I invited him to the EIHO.

"Bill, I really *like* Barry," the decision maker said. "He has all the qualities we're looking for, and I'm sure we're going to make him an offer."

"But I have to admit something to you," he said, almost apologetically. "If I had seen his resume before today, *I would never have wanted to interview him!"*

Dealing with the Resume Mentality

As a trainer, I'm often asked by other recruiters how to "overcome" the "resume objection." Here's my answer:

I don't try to overcome it. I try to *understand* the perceived need to see a resume, using client-centered selling techniques. You'd be amazed to learn some of the real reasons:

• *Force of habit.* Even *they* don't know why they want to see a resume, they've just been programmed to ask.

155

- *Recruiter screening.* They use the resume to screen *you,* not the candidate. They're afraid you're unfamiliar with their industry or needs, and ask for a sample resume to see if you're qualified to work with them.

- *Nosiness.* They're curious to see if your candidate is a person they know, or someone who works for their own company.

- *Foul play.* They want to steal your candidate and not pay you a fee.

- *Avoidance of the "no" word.* They have no interest in working with you, and don't know any other way to ask you to go away.

- *Honorable motives that are poorly communicated.* They simply want more information about your candidate. That's all.

The point is, there are so many reasons why a prospect might want to see a resume, it would be foolish to have a stock "rebuttal" prepared each time you meet with resistance.

The best way to handle the request for a resume is to channel the discussion in such a way that you begin to get a dialogue going. Soon, the prospect's need to see a resume may disappear altogether.

Naturally, your candidate should bring his resume to an interview. Not only is it a courtesy to the employer, there's a lot of useful information contained in a resume that will aid in getting an interview going.

But never, never, *never* make it a habit to automatically send resumes to your client for applicant screening, unless you're comfortable being a low billing recruiter. And please, use the fax machine for more productive things, like sending invoices!

One of the hardest things to do in our business is say "no." But believe me, any prospect that insists on a resume (or a discount, or that you work only with personnel) is waving a big red flag, and may not be much of a customer in the long run.

By enforcing consistent policies regarding fees, terms and conditions, you can sidestep a slew of recruiting minefields --- and dramatically increase your billings.

14

Carving Out a Market Niche

*T*here's practically no limit to the number of organizations that need your service. After all, *people* are the most fundamental asset to any business.

The old saying, "good help is hard to find" has never been more true, especially in light of the recent changes in demographics, our nation's deteriorating educational system, and global boom in service industry and technical jobs requiring a high level of skill and training.

The need for quality people is not restricted by an organization's size, profitability, product, service, or location.

Even non-profit institutions rely on search firms to help them fill critical positions.

However, we sometimes make assumptions that limit our perception of who our potential customers might be. Remember, our prospects are qualified by their ability to want, use, need, and afford our service.

For that reason, assuming that a company of three employees can't use your service because it lacks sufficient funds to pay a fee may cost you dearly. You may find the next time you call on them that your competitor has built that company into a major account. Similarly, organizations that are downsizing or manufacturing a mature product may desperately need your help; don't overlook them!

Looks Can be Deceiving

Ironically, I've found that in many cases the company that appears to have the least ability to afford your service cannot live without it.

To illustrate this paradox, let's examine two companies that manufacture girls' dresses. One of them is very large, the other very small. Which would you think has the greater ability to afford a $15,000 placement fee, the 100 million dollar company, or the one million dollar company?

Well, the answer is obvious: the one hundred million dollar company has more money to spend. But which one has the greater need?

Let's suppose the big company employs twelve production supervisors, and the little company employs one production supervisor. And it just so happens that one of the twelve supervisors at the big company breaks his leg at the very same time the only supervisor at the little company breaks his.

This misfortune couldn't occur at a worse time; both companies are in the midst of a heavy production run in preparation for fall distribution.

Now, which can least afford to be without a production supervisor, the big company with eleven others who can cover the job, or the little company who has no one else who knows the job or can handle the work?

Again, the answer is obvious.

This story helps explain a basic truth concerning the executive search market: *The smaller the client company, the greater the need for your service.*

True, the small companies may have to dig a little deeper to cover their costs, but in the long run, they're glad to have your help.

In contrast, I have found that companies or divisions that employ more than 300 people almost always complain about the fee, set the most rigid ground rules, impose the maximum number of unrealistic requirements, and act without the least sense of urgency.

Why? Because, like the 100 million dollar dress company, they usually have a duplication of job functions.

The client "sweet spot" of most high-billing recruiters is a cache of companies, each with less than three hundred employees. In those organizations, every single person counts, including you!

Who are Your Real Customers?

Each company is made up of unique individuals who collectively form an equally unique "corporate culture."

Since no two corporate cultures are exactly alike, you have to be flexible in the way you relate to different companies.

At the same time, you must be aware of who your *real* customers are. Within a client company, your contacts will fall into three categories: *decision makers, partial decision makers,* and *non-decision makers.*

It's always best to work with a decision maker, such as the company president, or hiring manager.

Partial decision makers might include hiring manager peers, higher authorities, or personnel managers.

Non-decision makers are those who have no authority when it comes to making a hiring decision, nor your role in the placement process (although they can be very valuable in helping you to form networks or gather information). Personnel administrators and hiring authorities' secretaries fall into this category. For the purpose of writing job orders and making deals, these people should be avoided.

Why? Because the first rule of selling is: *Don't take "no" from someone who can't say "yes."*

Non-decision makers can't say *yes.* Decision makers can.

It should come as no surprise, then, that high billing recruiters tend to work with decision makers. Low billing recruiters tend to work with non-decision makers and partial decision makers!

I once knew a low billing recruiter who habitually made presentations of his applicants to a decision maker's secretary. The poor fellow engaged in the most pitiful groveling I ever witnessed in his attempt to arrange sendouts.

You can bet the secretary enjoyed her feeling of power, but the recruiter hardly ever made any deals, and eventually his company had to let him go.

Does this mean that you should *never* work with anyone other than the hiring manager or company president? Not at all. Each company is unique, and you may occasionally make placements by forming productive relationships with partial decision makers, or even non-decision makers.

But high billing is impossible unless you consistently work with those who can say *yes.* The greater proportion of time you spend with qualified decision makers, the higher your billings will be!

Key Account Development

Given the choice of making ten placements with ten companies, or ten placements with three companies, which would you prefer?

I'd prefer working with three companies. Why?

First of all, those three companies have all given me repeat business. That means they're likely to again.

Second, from all the time I've spent working with them, I've become familiar with their nuances and corporate cultures. That means I don't have to reinvent the wheel with each job order. I have built-in rapport.

Ever heard of the 80/20 rule? It states that 80 percent of your income will come from 20 percent of your customers.

High billing recruiters usually have a high percentage of "key accounts," or companies they've nurtured and developed profitable working relationships with.

It's nearly impossible to achieve high billings if you're flitting from one company to the next.

Establish key accounts as the twenty percent of your customers, and they'll be certain to provide you with eighty percent of your income.

However, you need to make sure that you continue to market your service, since no one group of customers can sustain your billings indefinitely.

High billing recruiters carve out a specific
market niche and faithfully serve the
needs of their key client accounts.

15

Adopting and Sustaining a High-Billing Mentality

*O*ur attitudes are the combination of our feeling of self-worth and the assumptions we make about others. In this chapter, we'll examine how these attitudes can affect our business success.

As a recruiter, I've learned to make only three assumptions:

1] The world is made up of good, honest, ethical people who will treat you fairly.

2] Candidates and employers are generally receptive to friendly, well-meaning recruiters who have a sincere desire to help them get what they want.

3] Recruiters, by nature and necessity, are people who take responsibility for their actions. Therefore, their earnings are in direct proportion to the quality of the work they provide.

However, I've found that subscribing to too many preconceived ideas will eventually undermine a person's success.

Assumptions Can be Dangerous

For example, a few years back I had just begun to work on an assignment for a good client of mine, an electronics company in California.

I'd considered presenting my client's job opportunity to Milt, an applicant I knew, but decided not to.

You see, a year earlier, I'd spoken to Milt about a similar position with the same company, and he wasn't interested.

Why call Milt, I thought. *He wasn't interested then; he won't be interested now.*

Who do you think the company hired?

Milt.

Who do you suppose earned the fee?

Another recruiter. Of course.

I'm ashamed to admit this, but Milt and I go way back. Four years earlier, I had contacted Milt about a position, but failed to really explore it with him, because taking the position would have involved a relocation. So I let it slide.

Who do you think ended up relocating, and taking that same position a month later, through another recruiter?

Milt.

So, I lost two fees totaling $35,000 because I made assumptions.

It's Not Who You Know

I've also witnessed the negative effect assumptions can have on other recruiters, especially when they first get into the business.

Jerry came to work for my company, after having spent thirty years in the consumer electronics industry.

He knew *everybody,* or so he said. He had published an industry magazine. He had a booth at the annual trade show. He played golf in Palm Springs with all the heavy hitters. And on and on.

"This business is gonna be a snap," he told me, as he settled into the desk next to mine. "I'll just call up my buddies and let 'em know old Jerry's in the headhunting business."

Jerry lasted exactly one month with my company. His assumption that he knew *everybody* and that they'd want to do business with him drove him right out the door.

I know a training director for a large search firm who believes people are basically dishonest. "They all lie," he tells his new employees.

For me, it would simply be impossible to work happily and productively in the "people" business if that were true.

You're Worth the Money You Charge!

I can't tell you the number of times I've heard the expression, "fifty percent of something is better than 100 percent of nothing."

Hogwash!

Fifty percent is better only in a collection or bad debt crisis, when someone is cheating you out of what he owes you, and you feel lucky to recoup any part of your loss.

But caving in on a regular basis and accepting less than what your service is worth is not only costly in financial terms; it subconsciously "telegraphs" to your customer that you're not a believer in what you do for a living. Eventually, this kind of noncommittal attitude will harm your credibility, and weaken your earning potential.

Some years ago, I had a "fifty percent of something" experience that proved to be very painful in the short term, but beneficial in the long.

I cold called the vice president of a company and proceeded to market an extremely talented MPA.

"Bill, your candidate sounds like the sort of person we need," explained the vice president. "In fact, we're currently conducting a search.

"However, we're using a retained search firm on this assignment."

"So you're pleased with the results you're getting," I said.

"Well, not exactly. You're probably aware of how difficult it is to find someone like this."

"Indeed I am, Mr. Employer, and that's why I called you. What should we do?"

"Tell you what," said the vice president. "Why don't you talk to Leo, the other recruiter? Tell him the situation; that you have an ideal candidate I want to interview. Maybe the two of you can split the fee. See what he says, and call me back."

What could be the harm? I figured.

Sure enough, Leo was receptive to the idea. It turns out he wasn't getting anywhere on this assignment.

"How about it, Bill? You and I will split the fee fifty-fifty," suggested Leo. "That way, we'll both look good. And besides, fifty percent of something is better than one hundred percent of nothing, right?"

"Hmmm...I'm not sure," I hesitated. "Let me think about it and I'll call you back."

Now I was *really* confused! I went to my manager for advice.

"I'm sorry, Bill," he said, shaking his head, "but I can't approve a split deal like this."

"But it would mean walking away from a lot of money," I groaned. "And besides, there's no guarantee I can place my MPA anywhere else."

"That's just the risk you'll have to take," my manager replied. "You see, the issue here isn't the money. The issue is the value of your service."

"What do you mean?"

"Well, you took the initiative to cold call the employer and present your MPA, right?"

"Right."

"And he'd like to interview your MPA because he's perfect for the job."

"True," I said.

"Now, let's suppose you were to arrange the interview, and as a result, the company decided to hire your applicant.

"Haven't you done everything we teach you to do, and done it well?"

"Sure," I answered proudly.

"So aren't you entitled to 100 percent of the fee, and not a penny less?"

"I guess so."

"Now ask yourself this: What did Leo, the other recruiter, do to earn half your money?"

"Nothing," I muttered.

As I walked back to my desk, I thought about what my manager just told me.

He's right! Why should I give Leo half my fee, just because he happened to write a job order?

A few minutes later, I called the vice president.

"Mr. Employer," I said. "I spoke with Leo, as you suggested, and he offered to split the fee with me.

"But I've got some disappointing news for you. I thought it over, and I can't in good conscience give Leo half my fee. I just don't feel it would be fair."

"I don't blame you," said the vice president. "Leo shouldn't be rewarded for his failure to find me the right person. Unfortunately, I have to stick with Leo, because we signed an exclusive agreement, but I appreciate your calling me. Let's keep in touch."

"Fine. I'll call you in a few months."

Would you like to know how this story ended? Leo finally placed a marginal candidate with the vice president's company.

I stayed in touch with the company, and even made a courtesy call to meet the vice president.

Two years later, the candidate Leo placed was fired, and I was asked by the company to fill the vacant position, which I did, for a full fee.

The lesson I learned?

Once you've assumed a high-billing mentality, you'll never want to settle for less than you're worth!

16

Preparation Strategies for Higher Billings

*I*f you drive a car or own a home, then you know the importance of preventive maintenance.

Operating a profitable recruiting business also requires maintenance. For that reason, it's a good idea to have a "tool box" handy, both to keep things running smoothly, and to make minor adjustments when needed.

By far, the best tools for preventive maintenance are *checklists*. Checklists can take many forms. For example, your calendar is a form of checklist. Use it to set and follow up appointments and phone calls.

Another type of checklist is a "tickle file" that reminds you to call prospects, placed applicants, or clients on a regular basis.

A Day in the Life of a Checklist

I'm a big believer in checklists, because I feel they reduce stress, organize your time, and help you set priorities.

To manage a complex transaction in which the events are sequential, following a checklist becomes a necessity, not a luxury.

Consider for a moment the typical life cycle of a placement as it winds its way through the three phases. You'd be surprised at how many items there are to keep track of, and how easy they are to overlook.

I've italicized the checklist items to illustrate the number of steps we must follow to successfully complete a deal.

[1] The RECRUIT Phase

1]   Marketing call, job order lead, or repeat business results in a qualified, fillable, "real" job order.

2]   Recruit, screen, and *qualify* applicants.

3]   Present applicants to employer, and *requalify job order, handle any concerns, check search status, arrange interviews, prepare employer, and preclose.*

4]   *Thoroughly prepare applicants for the interview, handle any concerns, requalify, and preclose again. Also, make sure to explore their level of commitment and any red flags related to counteroffers or other interviews.*

5] After interview, *debrief applicants, handle concerns, preclose, get commitments on salary, start date.*

6] *Debrief employer, handle concerns, set up second interview, check for commitment to hire and for any further procedural matters, and check search status.*

7] *Thoroughly reference check applicant, paying particular attention to any concerns the employer might have.*

8] *Read references to employer and get commitment to hire.*

9] After second interview, *debrief applicant.*

10] *Close applicant on acceptance, salary, title, start date. Get his permission for you to accept on his behalf.*

11] *Debrief employer, checking search status.*

[2] The OFFER Phase

1] *Close employer on intention to hire.*

2] *Close employer on salary, title, and start date which are acceptable to the applicant.*

3] *Accept offer on behalf of applicant, and congratulate employer for a job well done.*

4]   *Call applicant and congratulate him.*

5]   *Have the applicant call the employer and accept personally, reiterating the title, salary, and start date.*

[3] The TRANSITION Phase

1]   *Prepare applicant for resignation; and work to overcome his feelings of buyer's remorse. Also, reinforce his decision to accept.*

2]   *Help arrange for any outside services if needed, such as Realtors, spousal placement, relocation assistance, or travel needs.*

3]   *Get employer involved by having him assign the applicant a project, or take the applicant to lunch.*

4]   *Monitor applicant's mood and actions after resignation.*

5]   *Visit the job site after the applicant starts, and take him and the employer to lunch.*

6]   *Stay in touch with the employer and the applicant.*

7]   *Write a new job order!*

Even the most experienced recruiters need help in remembering all these items, especially if other deals are in progress. That's why we keep checklists. Like the batter who has just hit a home run in the game of baseball, we need to tag every base in sequence, or the umpire may call us out.

Breaking Murphy's Law

To illustrate the need for following a checklist, I once had a applicant and an employer who really wanted to work with each other. All that was left in order for the deal to come together was for the employer to call the references and make the offer.

I was so impressed by the applicant when I first interviewed him that I never bothered to check his references. Ever heard of Murphy's Law?

Sure enough, the employer received some negative feedback on the applicant, and declined to make the offer.

And the deal died.

Later, I called the person who had given the negative feedback and found that he wasn't even a credible reference for the applicant. He was a prima donna with an ax to grind, and wasn't the least bit qualified to pass judgment.

But it was too late; the damage had been done. If only I had called the reference prior to the employer, and immediately notified the employer that the applicant would get a discredited reference, I would have had a deal.

Who was it that really killed the deal? Me. I had become lazy, and didn't follow my checklist.

That's why it's so important to refer to the checklists in your tool box, the same way an airline pilot checks every instrument and gauge in the cockpit before taking off down the runway. By the time you're in the air, it may be too late to fix a problem.

The Value of Interview Preparation

There's no denying the importance of thoroughly preparing an applicant for an interview with your client.

175

By conceptualizing an applicant's preparation as a three-step process and following a checklist, you can greatly enhance the odds of a successful interview.

1] *Preframe*. Provide the applicant with all the information you can about the job function, company, product, interviewer, and so forth.

You should also let him know what the interviewer's expectations are, the status of the search, and the company's time frame for making a decision.

Confirm with the applicant his interview location, date, time, and correct name and title of the interviewer.

Let the applicant know that most employers do everything they can to make interviews comfortable and enjoyable. If your applicant is feeling tense, let him know that as the interview progresses, he will begin to relax.

2] *Preview*. Discuss with the applicant the way he should conduct himself during a job interview.

Cover important issues such as appropriate attire, punctuality, and politeness.

Have the applicant bring a couple of copies of his resume, and ask him to please *read* his resume before the interview.

Remind the applicant to answer the employer's questions thoroughly and completely, and to recognize the difference between questions that require a short answer and a long, detailed answer.

Strongly suggest that the applicant avoid asking questions about the position's salary, or company benefits, especially on a first interview.

When asked about current salary, tell the applicant to answer honestly, and to mention any upcoming bonuses, raises, or perquisites that are part of his compensation.

In response to the specific question, "What are you looking to earn in a new position," have the applicant answer by giving the employer a *range,* such as "low to mid-forties," or "high forties to low fifties."

Make sure the applicant shows enthusiasm for his work, and for the new position, in order to maximize his chances of getting an offer.

3] *Preclose.* Always ask the applicant if there's anything standing in the way of his accepting an offer and starting in two weeks, provided the interview goes well, and the company makes a fair offer.

Encourage the applicant to ask for the job, if he is sincerely excited about the opportunity to work for your client.

Although I prefer the "partnership" role to the "coach" role when preparing an applicant for an interview, there is a specific script I give an applicant to use when there is sincere interest by both the employer and the applicant.

At the conclusion of the interview, I rehearse the applicant to use this exact line:

"Well, Mr. Employer, this job looks *very* good to me. Can you think of any reason why we can't just put this deal together right now, and have me start in two weeks?"

Depending on the employer's response, you'll either have a placement, or an exact reading on where you and the applicant stand.

Standardizing Your Written Communications

Surprise! Your *applicant* is on the line, and he's got some good news to tell you. It seems your client offered him a job at the interview this morning, and he accepted on the spot!

Your applicant wants to submit his letter of resignation this afternoon. Can you help him write it?

Sure, but he'll have to hold on, you've got a call on the other line.

It's your *client*. He'd like you to put the applicant's references in the mail to complete their files.

He also wants to know how to properly word his company's letter of offer.

Just a minute. You've got another call coming in.

Oh, hello. It's the *runner-up applicant*. It seems your client was very encouraging at this morning's interview, and he wants the runner-up applicant to stay in touch.

Could you help draft a thank-you note?

Sure, but it'll have to wait. You've got an appointment in ten minutes with a *prospective client*, and it seems you've misplaced the three letters of recommendation you promised you'd give him.

Letters, letters, letters! They all want letters!

This is why you keep *form letters* handy.

Form letters can be used over and over again. They can even be dictated over the phone, or faxed.

Naturally, there will be variations in *content,* but the *form* will remain the same.

Letters in the Tool Box

To be adequately prepared for the unexpected, your tool box should contain the following documents:

- A standard letter of resignation;

- A standard letter of offer;

- A standard format for an applicant's references;

- A standard thank-you note; and

- A set of letters from clients recommending your service.

One useful trick I've learned is how to convert an employer's letter of *offer* into a letter of *acceptance*.

Instead of beginning the letter with the usual phrase, "We are pleased to offer you the position of vice president...," have the employer substitute the following:

"This letter confirms your acceptance of our offer..."

That way, everyone's commitment is solidified, and the wording acts as a safeguard against the applicant using your employer's letter as leverage against another company's offer.

Third-Party Relocation Specialists

Unless you have the proper tools, an applicant's relocation can present some major problems.

Recruiters often rely on "quality of life" surveys and statistics regarding geographic wage differentials and housing costs in an effort to "sell" an applicant on a given location.

However, I've found a different approach to handling an applicant's concerns regarding a prospective relocation: I simply call in the experts: the people known as *relocation specialists*.

Relocation specialists are brokers who make their living by matching applicants and *locations*, similar to the way recruiters match applicants and *employers*.

Relocation specialists interview applicants (and their spouses) who wish to relocate. They discover their housing and lifestyle needs, and then refer them to Realtors who are familiar with the applicant's preferred location. Relocation specialists receive a commission (or finder's fee) from the Realtor, once a property is sold. There is no charge to you, the applicant, or your client.

In the event you're unable to find a relocation specialist in a particular geographic area, then you can turn to a Realtor, provided the Realtor has significant experience in relocation, rather than cross-town house-hunting.

In many cases, relocation specialists will prequalify applicants for mortgage loans, and refer applicants to amenable loan officers or lending institutions.

Relocation specialists are also good at handling unusual situations.

For instance, a relocation specialist I was working with was able to help an applicant's wife transfer her teaching credential from California to Michigan. Without the transfer, the applicant would not have been able to accept my client's offer.

In another instance, a relocation specialist was able to pinpoint the exact housing needs of an applicant and his wife, show them the perfect property, qualify them, and arrange a five percent down mortgage loan with a bank, all in one morning! That afternoon, the applicant went to his final interview with my client and accepted an offer, secure in the knowledge that his relocation wouldn't be a problem.

If you haven't done so already, cultivate a good working relationship with several good relocation specialists, and keep their names and numbers in your tool box, because relocation specialists will help you close more deals.

The success of every high billing recruiter is built on a bedrock of organization, efficiency and preparation.

Fig. 16.1 Candidate marketing logs are essential to your desk organization and allow you to catalog your marketing efforts.

Radin Associates Candidate Marketing Log

Candidate _____ Current Employer/Position _____

Date	(✔)	Company/Contact	Remarks/Interview

Fig. 16.2 The sheer amount of search data can overwhelm you, unless you can efficiently chronicle your call activity.

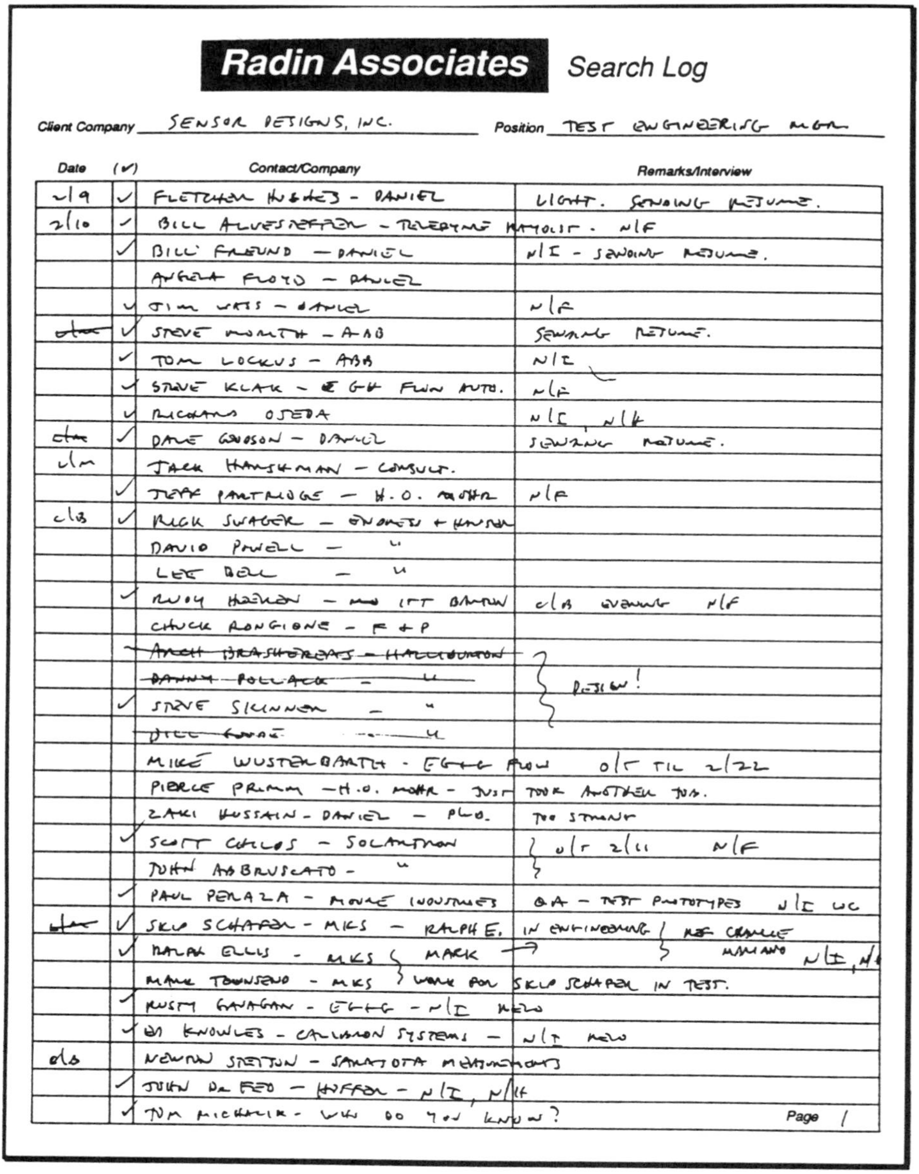

17

Advanced Marketing Strategies

*M*odern recruiting technology divides the professional working population into four categories. With the exception of a few "borderline" jobs, each person's occupation will fit into one of these groups:

1] *Technical* includes those people with skills in engineering, scientific research, chemistry, testing, manufacturing, production, quality control, plant management, drafting, and so on.

2] *Sales* refers to those who earn their living by selling any sort of product or service. This can include real estate, plastics, consumer products, bonds, insurance, and so forth. A borderline job would be technical sales, in which a requirement for the position would be an engineering degree.

3] *Electronic data processing (EDP)* refers to data processing *(or information systems* or *IS)* professionals such as programmers, MIS managers, systems analysts, and the like. Borderline groups would be [1] manufacturing engineers who program the complex numerical controls of machine tools; or [2] those in the computer industry who call themselves "software engineers."

4] *Administration* falls into two groups: those who administer the work of others (such as contract administrators or general managers); or those working in the following industries or skill specialties: banking, real estate, insurance, law, health care, retail, hospitality, advertising, personnel, finance or accounting. Borderline jobs would be purchasing, marketing, or traffic and distribution.

Subsets of these categories help to refine your perception of each candidate. Think of a person as having a *title or function,* a *skill or application,* or an affiliation with a *product or service.*

For example, a controller (title) with a public accounting background (skill) might be employed by a toy manufacturer (product). The same company might also employ an electrical engineer (title) who designs production equipment (skill), as well as a sales representative (title) who sells exclusively to the retail industry (skill), and a systems analyst (title), who is an IBM system 36 specialist (skill).

Defining Your Desk Specialty

Now let's pinpoint the specific market you wish to serve.

The most effective way to define your market, or *desk specialty*, is by working within a category and one or more subsets (for example, ADMIN: retail, SALES: chemicals, EDP: micros, or TECH: valves).

After a few search assignments, your focus will become more concentrated, and your contacts and files will assume a greater degree of continuity. At this point, you will want to eliminate unrelated subsets and add complimentary subsets to your desk specialty. This will help you to clearly identify the scope of your operation.

Typical desk specialty market niches might include:

- TECH. Subset being engineers (title), who design electrical circuits (skill), for computer manufacturers (product).

- SALES. Subset being salespeople (title), selling to distributors (skill), specializing in home appliances (product).

- EDP. Subset being programmers (title) with RPG II experience (skill), who work for hospitals (product or service).

- ADMIN: Subset being accountants (title), with experience in audit (skill), who have experience with small to medium size manufacturers (product).

Unless you live in a rural area, and want to restrict yourself to serving the needs of your community, try to avoid working in too many categories and subsets so as not to become generalized.

Careful planning is required to expand your area of expertise into another market -- so exercise caution when taking on assignments in unrelated fields. You will risk losing focus and continuity, while spending time building files in isolated fields which have nothing in common.

I knew someone with a data processing desk specialty who got sidetracked by working job orders for positions in the hospitality and advertising industries. Guess how many placements she made in those areas? None.

One of the craziest things I ever did was try to develop a niche in the plumbing industry after filling a call-in job order for a plumbing plant manager (my specialty was electronics). I figured that since I made one quick placement in plumbing, more would soon follow.

Unfortunately, all I ended up doing was building files in an unrelated subset. Since I couldn't present my plumbing candidates to my electronics clientele (or vice versa), my efforts resulted in a complete waste of time.

Maintaining Related, Peripheral Markets

As important as it is to specialize in order to build a healthy business, it's equally important not to *overspecialize*.

Since all industries experience fluctuations, use the added subset approach to nurture *related,* peripheral markets. This will protect your desk from any unexpected dips in your industry.

If you concentrate in personal computer sales placement, for example, you might want to develop a need for your services with companies that manufacture other types of consumer electronics, such as stereo equipment, calculators, games and toys, or similar products.

Salary Range: Finding Your Sweet Spot

Salaries can vary greatly, depending on geography, industry, title, and so on. You want to work with candidates whose earnings fall within the accepted ranges in their field, as well as the boundaries of ours.

Secretarial and office support personnel tend to earn in the $15,000 to $35,000 range, while the contingency executive search boundaries extend from $30,000 to $80,000 and beyond.

Because there's a greater need for people at the lower salary levels, it makes sense to concentrate in this range initially. Later, when you want to expand your market, move into the higher income brackets. In any case, try to work within a salary "sweet spot," similar to the way you work within your desk specialty.

Here are some examples of salary sweet spots:

• Project engineers: 35k to 50k

• District sales managers: 50k to 75K

• Programmer/analysts: 35k to 55k

• Hospital administrators: 45k to 60k

Naturally, each employment market will set its own salary levels. For example, the prevailing rate of pay for a biogeneticist in Indiana may get only a yawn from a similarly skilled candidate in New Jersey.

Increasing Your Market Visibility

It stands to reason that expanding your pool of potential customers will enable you to make more sales, provided you can discover and satisfy needs.

In addition to putting your name in front of more prospects, increasing your market visibility will enhance your credibility among those within the industry you serve.

The best way to increase your visibility is simply to do good work, and build up a network of referrals.

Here are some other ways:

- *Visit your clients*. Your presence within their domain will be felt by other potential applicants and decision makers.

- *Join professional associations and societies*. The people within your desk specialty tend to belong to groups that focus on continued education or political action. If at all possible, you should join up and attend their meetings and lectures. The people you meet will respond warmly to your interest, and will be receptive to working with you.

- *Publish articles in trade journals*. The added visibility will enable you to open doors that otherwise may have been closed.

- *Attend trade shows and conventions*. By so doing, you not only stay abreast of the latest developments in your area of specialization, you also get the chance to cultivate new friendships and visit with old acquaintances.

A few years ago at a trade show in Cleveland, I happened to run into two people I hadn't seen in quite some time.

One was the general manager of a small company; the other, an engineering manager of a medium sized company.

They both asked me to call them the following week.

Each of them had search assignments for me, and both assignments resulted in placements a few weeks later.

I've found that one day's work at a trade show or convention is equivalent to a week on the phone.

Mass Mail Marketing Strategies

Using the telephone to market your service is by far the most effective way to establish your credibility, increase your visibility, and write job orders.

However, the use of mass mail marketing is also effective, and can supplement your billings considerably.

Once a piece of marketing literature is in your prospect's hands, your cold call suddenly becomes a "warm" call, because the prospect is already familiar with your name and the service you provide.

There are five basic types of mailings you can use:

1] A *generic* mailing, in which you simply send a letter, a business card or your company's brochure;

2] A *letter of congratulations* to a recently promoted decision maker, in which you emphasize your ability to help him staff his new department;

3] An *industry standout letter* that highlights the benefits and qualifications of a single MPA;

4] A *talent scout announcement,* or group MPA letter that lists five or six most placeable applicants and provides their capsule resumes; or

5] A *thank-you letter* that acknowledges the prospect's professional help with respect to a recent search assignment, candidate referral or reference check information.

These mailing strategies, particularly the last four, will greatly widen your business horizons, and deepen your penetration into the industry you serve.

The EIO: A Powerful Marketing Tool

Here's an advanced marketing technique you can use to capitalize on an upcoming EIO (Employer In Office).

Simply call a prospective employer and let him know when the EIO is going to occur, and encourage him to participate.

Refer to the EIO as a *staffing center,* and make the following presentation:

Recruiter: Mr. Employer, I'm calling to let you know about something you'll find very interesting.

One of your competitors has asked me to conduct a search for a sales manager with specific experience in your industry.

I've worked very hard, and I've found four extremely qualified candidates.

I've arranged for a staffing center to be held in my office next Wednesday, at which my client will prescreen the candidates individually. Each interview will last approximately thirty minutes.

> All of the candidates are quite capable, so it's just a matter of my client choosing the one he likes best, based on personality.
>
> It seems a shame to have so much talent in one office, and only one position available.
>
> For that reason, I'd like to give you the opportunity to attend the staffing center as well, and meet the candidates.
>
> What are your thoughts?

This approach is bound to create a great deal of interest, since you are presenting a situation to the employer which is full of potential *benefits*.

Even if the employer cannot attend, you have done much to establish your credibility, since you have demonstrated the capacity to find candidates for the employer's competitor.

Obviously, you have much to gain from marketing an EIO, since every additional employer in attendance increases your likelihood of making a placement.

I once piggybacked an EIO on top of an EIHO (Employer In His Office) by having all the EIO candidates meet me back at my office later in the day to interview with another employer.

Although I was able to make only one placement from both staffing centers, the experience turned out to be worthwhile, since I opened many new doors as a result of the unique way in which I was able to market my service.

Print Advertising: Taking the Newspaper Route

Many recruiters use newspaper and magazine ads in order to generate new business.

By and large, print advertising attracts many more applicants than it does employers. If you're in an applicant-driven market or economy, then there's an obvious benefit to this strategy. Advertising your services in print increases your visibility, and legitimizes your business.

However, print advertising can often backfire, and have the same effect as opening a can of tomato juice on a white Berber carpet. Once the juice is spilled, it becomes a nightmare trying to clean up the mess.

A case in point: A few years back, I decided to list my executive search services in the *Directory of Executive Recruiters*, also known in the trade as the "red book" because of the color of its cover.

The red book is sold to employers and business libraries as a resource book for retained recruiters; the supposition being, if you're a hiring manager or HR director, you can pull out the red book and find a recruiter who serves your market niche.

Fine. I listed my service thusly:

Industry: Electronic sensors and instrumentation.
Positions: Engineering and sales management only.

And here's what happened. Over a two-year period, I received exactly two inquiries about my service from employers, which was all I really expected.

Unfortunately, the response was overwhelming from applicants. I use the word *unfortunately* because over the same two-year period, I received an average of ten unsolicited resumes a *day* (and usually a couple of phone calls for good measure) from job-seekers who had no association whatever with my clearly stated market specialty.

I really felt badly for the people who contacted me, because they were only doing what any motivated job-seeker should do: find any available resource and "crash the boards."

However, neither the job hunters nor myself were served by this approach, because I'm in no position to help lingerie designers, international investment bankers or fertilizer executives. The hundreds of unsolicited applicants who felt the need to call me or send their resumes were just wasting their time (and mine).

So, I had to cancel my listing because of the nuisance it created. I can't fault Kennedy Publications, because their red book is an important resource in the employment industry. I suspect that their list of recruiters somehow found its way to at least one on-line service, which in turn disseminated the information in a way that got out of control.

A better approach to print advertising is to list your services in the specialized trade magazines that serve your niche-market constituency. You may not get the "pull" that you would in a generic publication, but at least your inquiries will be much more qualified.

In any case,

The more techniques you use to penetrate your market, the greater your billings will become.

Fig. 17.1 A strong marketing letter written to a hiring authority can often lead to an inquiry --- and a new business partnership.

January 2, 1996

Mr. Richard Caust
RUNWAY TECHNOLOGIES
3400 Garcia Pike
Los Lunas, NM 87222

Dear Richard:

I appreciate your taking the time to serve as a professional reference for Ted Greene. Your help is extremely valuable in a confidential search assignment, and I appreciate your input.

Radin Associates is a niche-market executive search firm that specializes in the sensor industry. Since 1985, we've earned a reputation for integrity, quality service, and above all, results.

At some point in time, you'll want to add a high-achieving sales professional, manager, or innovative engineer to your staff.

And when you do, we hope you'll choose Radin Associates to locate and capture the industry talent you need.

Sincerely,

William G. Radin, President
RADIN ASSOCIATES

WGR: rbl/Enclosure

18

Goal Achievement Strategies for Recruiters

$\mathcal{T}$he basic principles of goal achieving are fairly straightforward. Goals must be measurable, time-bounded, and realistic.

In the search business, each of the keys to peak performance can become the target of goal achieving strategies.

You're already increasing your *knowledge* by reading this book, and are no doubt thinking of ways to improve your *congruence*.

So let's focus on achieving *action* goals that will raise your billings.

The Pursuit of Measurable Activity

The following is a flow chart that accurately explains productivity in our business:

- Your Income is the result of placements.

- Placements are the result of sendouts.

- Sendouts are the result of job orders.

- Job orders are the result of marketing your service.

- All of the above are made possible by phone calls.

Placements, sendouts, job orders, and telephone marketing are what I refer to as *measurable activity*.

Gabbing with your in-laws, filing unsolicited resumes, arranging social functions and collecting bets for the interoffice fantasy football league are meaningless activities, at least with respect to earning a living.

Speaking of fantasy football, I worked in an office a few years back that was really into sports.

Actually, *obsessed* would have been a better word.

I swear to God, more time and energy was spent calculating batting averages, RBIs and slugging percentages than was ever spent arranging interviews, debriefing candidates or putting deals together. The compulsive nature of the office (and the total lack of focus on recruiting) got so bad, I had to quit.

Which brings me to my point: The more you increase your measurable activity, the more you increase your billings, or personal income.

Achieving a Goal Orientation

Before you set goals for future performance, take a look at your current level of production, based on what you've achieved over the last twelve months. Your *production data* can be easily quantified, in terms of:

- Personal income;

- Number of placements;

- Average number of sendouts per week;

- Average number of job orders written per week;

- Average number of daily outgoing phone calls;

- Sendout to placement ratio;

- Job order to placement ratio;

- "Hot Sheet" closure percentage (the number of deals you close after the applicant has gone to a second interview); and

- "Misery Index," or percentage of deals which result in falloffs, turndowns, or accepted counteroffers.

Now that you've collected your production data, which of these four categories best describes your work?

1] The *high billing, high activity* recruiter: You produce a consistent flow of high quality activity, make a lot of placements, and rarely experience a slump.

2] The *high billing, low activity* recruiter: You are a *sharpshooter* who has periods of billing peaks and valleys, due to a lack of sustained activity.

3] The *low billing, high activity* recruiter: You have lots of job orders and/or sendouts, but very few deals.

4] The *low billing, low activity* recruiter: You are just getting started in the business, or you are in a slump (or have decided, consciously or unconsciously, to leave the business).

If you have high billings and lots of activity, then increasing production is merely a matter of doing more of what has already made you successful. Many people in this category set goals relating to their quality of life, or increasing efficiency, or improving their managerial skills. Basically, you are in the driver's seat, with lots of options as to where to guide your career.

If you have high billings but low activity, you need to increase your number of weekly job orders and sendouts. This will automatically increase your production, since your competency is not a serious issue; you have already relied on it to get you this far.

If you have lots of activity, but are struggling to maintain or improve production, you should concentrate on raising your *competency* to increase your billings. Talk to other recruiters, read books, listen carefully to tapes, and by all means, consult with your manager.

If you have low numbers and low production, you need to raise your competency and level of activity. You might also make an honest exploration of your feelings of *congruence* in regards to a career in the personnel placement business.

Setting Realistic Goals

We've just measured your production, within a time frame of the previous twelve months.

Is it realistic to set a goal of doubling or tripling your income in the next twelve month period?

I don't think so. A more realistic goal would be to increase your productivity by up to fifty percent.

Simply take the numbers for the last twelve months, and calculate where you want to be twelve months from now, in order to set your new goal.

Competency and congruence goals are difficult to track, unless you can quantify the results, or the methods you use to achieve them.

On the other hand, activity goals are easily set and measured.

For example, it sounds ridiculously simple, but one of the best ways to increase your income is to increase the number of phone calls you make.

That is, if you billed $100,000 last year, and made thirty phone calls a day, you can bill $150,000 this year by making forty-five phone calls a day.

In fact, you'll probably do even better than that, since your level of competency will also increase by virtue of your experience.

Naturally, you can concentrate on improving other areas of meaningful activity, such as writing more job orders, or increasing the number of weekly sendouts, if you discover the need to do so.

The trick is to *quantify* all your meaningful activity, since what gets measured gets done.

Practical Goal-Setting Methodologies

The various aspects of your life are interrelated, and for the purpose of goal setting, can be classified into three groups: professional, personal and self-improvement.

The concept of congruence is particularly important when embarking on a goal achieving mission. For example, it's unlikely that you can achieve a $200,000 billing goal next year if your personal goal is to sail around the world in a kayak, beginning next week.

Make your goals clear, specific, realistic, and time-bounded for best results; and remember to share them only with those who are also committed to achieving goals.

The following (fig. 18.1) is a journal of goal achieving, used by a hypothetical recruiter named Cal Collins. You can add or delete specific objectives, depending on the measurable improvements you want to make. For our purposes, we'll concentrate only on Cal's professional goals, which are quantifiable and represent an ambitious yet achievable increase of 50 percent.

As you can see, Cal used a 12-month calendar year period as a unit of measure, but you can convert it to quarters, months, or even weeks, if you so desire.

Notice the way Cal set his goals? First, he measured his current activity, then extrapolated his numbers so that his personal income would rise proportional to his productivity.

Cal's next step (see fig. 18.2) will be to commit to writing the meaning behind his goals, and the ways in which their achievement will change his life. He will also be required to identify any methods for helping him reach his goals, and make mention of the specific people he can count on to provide support and reinforcement.

200

Fig. 18.1 A goal achieving strategy forces you to track and predict measurable activity --- and its corresponding billings.

Journal of Goal Achieving

Part 1. Recruiter's Professional Activity

Name _CAL COLLINS_ Today's date _1-5-96_

Previous time period _1-1-95_ to _12-31-95_

New time period _1-1-96_ to _12-31-96_

- Instructions: Compare your new goals with those you achieved during the previous time period.

Goal	Last period	[Actual]	New period
1. Personal income:	$ 40,000	$46,800	$60,000
2. Yearly billings:	$100,000	$117,000	$150,000
3. Quarterly billings:	$ 25,000	$ 29,250	$ 37,500
4. Yearly placements:	10	12	15
5. Weekly sendouts:	2	2.4	3
6. Weekly job orders:	2	2.3	3
7. Daily outgoing calls:	30	37	45
8. Quarterly EIOs:	1	1.2	1.5
9. Weekly recruited MPAs:	1	1.8	2

- Agreement: The goals listed above are realistic, achievable, and time-bounded; and I hereby commit myself to achieving them.

- Signature: _Cal Collins_

Monitoring Your Goals

Be sure to accurately record your activity. For example, if you average 3.4 sendouts per week, use that as your measure of production, not a rounded-off number.

Regardless of the frequency of your overall goal-setting, you should carefully monitor your progress on a regular basis. It does little good to set a "goal" in which progress is measured intermittently, or infrequently.

When I was working a desk in Los Angeles in the 1980s, the first thing I did every morning (even before I got to the coffee pot) was look at the number of phone calls I made the day before. (We had an automated system that allowed us to monitor all sorts of useful telephone statistics.)

If you set weekly sendout or job order goals, then by all means, monitor them weekly; don't wait until the end of the quarter. Only by staying current can you hope to accurately follow your plan.

It's been estimated that only three percent of the population sets specific goals for themselves and commits their goals to writing.

I have no idea how many recruiters faithfully set and achieve billing and professional goals, but my experience has shown that high billing recruiters are habitual goal achievers.

> High billing recruiters are
> invariably obsessed with goals
> and goal achieving.

Fig. 18.2 Successful goal achieving requires an examination of your motivation, commitment and ability to delay gratification.

Journal of Goal Achieving

Part 2. Recruiter's Self-Examination (confidential)

Name _____ Today's date _____

Previous time period _____ to _____

New time period _____ to _____

• Instructions: Please answer the following questions as honestly as possible, and share them only with your direct supervisor and/or other goal achievers.

1.   What will it mean to me to reach my personal income goal?

2.   How will the achievement of this goal affect my lifestyle? My quality of life? My relationships? My self-concept? My career?

3.   What specific methods will I use to reach my sendout, job order, EIO, and MPA recruiting goals?

4.   What additional hours must I work or changes to my lifestyle must I make in order to achieve my goals?

5.   What different tactics or strategies must I employ in order to achieve my goals? What new markets must I penetrate?

6.   What will it mean if I fail to reach my goals?

7.   What measures must I take if I find that I am falling short of my goals?

8.   Who can I call upon to encourage me, and reinforce my commitment to set and achieve goals?

9.   Are there any negative influences or specific individuals that might derail my efforts to achieve my goals?

10.   Is there anything preventing me from achieving my goals?

203

19

The Real Recruiters: Stories of Success

I've been privileged to know some people who have done extremely well for themselves in the field of executive search.

Terri, Paul, Toni, and Mike came from extraordinarily diverse backgrounds before becoming top-billing recruiters.

In their former lives, they were an English teacher, a rock-n-roll drummer, an experimental psychologist, and a social worker assigned to the congregation of a reform temple!

All of them rose quickly to become successful account executives, helping satisfy the needs of dozens of applicants and employers.

As a result of their efforts, each of them earned in excess of $100,000 per year in personal income within a few years of entering the business.

What was it that led to their success? Were they that much smarter, or harder working, or better connected than the average recruiter? Not at all.

They simply honed their powers of perception (the way they looked at the business) and utilized the three keys to peak performance to unleash their potential for success!

Three Keys to Peak Performance

Peak performance in our business is a matter of combining three complimentary keys: knowledge, action, and congruence.

1] *Knowledge* refers to your mastery of recruiting methodologies, and fundamental, or basic selling skills.

As you know, there are no "tricks" to this business, only the execution and perfection of the basics. As Vince Lombardi once said, the more "brilliant on the basics" you are, the better your results. When I find that something has gone wrong, I can almost always trace it to something very basic that I've neglected to do.

That's why I keep a card on my desk reminding me always to stay *brilliant on the basics.*

If you're new to the business, and just beginning to learn your chosen desk specialty, have faith; you'll come up to speed quickly.

Remember, you don't have to design monolithic circuits in order to place people who do. But you'd better be prepared to spend time boning up on your specialty in order to gain insight and credibility.

Possession of a broad, general knowledge is also valuable. Being well rounded allows you to build rapport and gain respect through common interests. It also aids in strengthening your overall trade skills, since business parallels life. I have found that the reading of biographies has been a consistent source of inspiration over the years, as they allow me to model myself after successful individuals. (Evidently, the people who came up with the "Ben Franklin" close were equally inspired!)

2] *Action* can take on many forms; it need not be flamboyant. The quiet determination of research, a tireless series of marketing calls, the relentless day and night recruiting to meet a deadline, and the application of a newly learned selling technique are all understated, yet positive actions which must occur on a routine basis.

There's no substitute for action; productivity in this business will simply not exist without your own initiative.

3] *Congruence* is the term which defines the relationship between your self-concept and your environment, daily activities, and long term goals.

Congruence is like the axle upon which the wheels of knowledge and action turn: it's what drives your success vehicle. Absolutely critical to your business, it would be unthinkable not to recognize its impact; yet surprisingly, the importance of congruence is often overlooked.

Each of us has a unique combination of personal beliefs, interests, aptitudes, physical abilities, and so forth. These and countless other elements in our conscious and subconscious minds define our self-concept, or *values.*

Asking the Right Questions

The degree to which these values are in "synch" with the way you spend your time (and with whom) will determine your level of congruency.

Ask yourself these questions: What is most important to me in life? In a job? In a relationship? What are my key, unshakable personal and spiritual beliefs? What are my feelings toward other people? What activities do I enjoy? What situations do I like being in? What makes me feel terrific? What makes me feel lousy? What am I good at professionally?

If the answers to these questions produce a feeling that's in harmony with the activities and objectives of a career in recruiting, that's great; you're experiencing a *congruent* lifestyle.

Have you ever known a person who hated his job? Stop and think what must be producing this feeling. It's a result of the job being *incongruent* with the person's values, or self-concept. The tragedy is that so many people allow themselves to exist in this mode.

On the other hand, a person who loves his work does so because it's congruent with his beliefs, interests, and feelings. Congruence is fundamental to job satisfaction and performance; and it eliminates the self-conflict which is so limiting and destructive.

I've found that there's hardly anyone in the world who *can't* do our job; it's just that there are relatively few who *will.* To me, the difference is a matter of congruence.

A major breakthrough for me came as a direct result of my rethinking the business in a manner which was consistent with my values. Not only did my income rise dramatically, I became much more relaxed and confident in my abilities, knowing that what I did and said came from the heart.

Your task, then, is to continually analyze your self-concept and the way it meshes with your career as a recruiter. Chances are you'll learn to appreciate your job and continue to grow with it, not fight it. And developing your skill at analyzing self-concept will prove particularly useful in helping understand other people's values.

The Recruiter as Triathlete

Now that you recognize the three keys to peak performance, I hope you'll begin to picture yourself as a triathlete.

Recruiting is very much like competing in a triathlon, a race which consists of three grueling events.

First, you have to run. Then you have to ride a bike and swim. If you can run and ride a bike, but can't swim, you can't qualify as a triathlete and compete in the race. (Of course, if you can run or ride a bike on water, you should be doing something else for a

The point is, like a triathlete, all three keys must come into play in order to successfully run the race: knowledge, action, and congruence. Try utilizing any combination of two without the other, such as action and congruence without knowledge, or action and knowledge without congruence, and you'll quickly see how limited your career potential will become.

High billing recruiters apply knowledge
through meaningful action in a manner
congruent with their self-concept.

Bill Radin • Billing Power!

20

Conclusion: Tracking the Ninja Recruiter

I could go on and on about what it takes to be a first-rate recruiter; but the best way to learn is by the example of others.

Therefore, I think it would only be fitting to conclude *Billing Power!* with a story about Mike, my former manager, and why he can be called a *Ninja* recruiter.

Like a Ninja, he's fearless, and works with lightning speed. And he's one of the most clever people I've ever met.

Wouldn't you say those are some of the qualities of a Ninja warrior?

The Marketing Call

One day, Mike was on the phone, marketing an MPA.

Mike's office was in Los Angeles, and his MPA lived in Los Angeles, but Mike decided to call a prospective employer in San Francisco.

Mike was thirty seconds into his MPA presentation when the employer interrupted him.

"Mike," said the employer, "your applicant sounds terrific, but I've already got my pick of good people."

"How's that?" asked Mike.

"Another search firm has set up a staffing center for me tomorrow, and I'll be looking at half a dozen people."

Hmmm, an EIO, thought Mike. *Pretty clever.*

"Well, certainly it wouldn't hurt to look at one more person, would it?" asked Mike.

"Not at all. In fact, your applicant sounds pretty interesting. The problem is, I'm going to be out of town."

"No kidding. Where will you be?"

"I'll be in Los Angeles," said the employer, "interviewing at the other search firm's office."

"Really," replied Mike. "Who's picking you up at the airport?"

"Well, no one. I was going to take a cab."

"Tell you what," said Mike. "I happen to live in Los Angeles. If it's okay with you, I'll pick you up at the airport, drop you off at the other search firm's office, and give you a ride back after your interviews are over.

"How does that sound?"

"Sounds better than taking a cab," replied the employer.

A Back Seat Surprise

Sure enough, the next morning Mike picked up the employer at the airport. As they drove to the other search firm's office, Mike asked a lot of questions about the employer's company, and the type of person the employer wanted to hire.

Later that day, after the "staffing center" was over, Mike was waiting in his car for the employer.

Only he wasn't alone.

He had his MPA in the back seat!

"Mr. Employer, I just couldn't let you pass up the opportunity to meet my MPA, since the two of you are so well matched," said Mike. "I'm sure you'll have a lot to talk about on the way to the airport."

Mike had hit the nail on the head. In fact, the two of them got along famously.

When they got to the airport, the employer insisted on taking Mike and the MPA to dinner. They got so involved in their conversation that the employer missed his flight, and had to take a later one.

The next day, the employer had the applicant flown up to his San Francisco office, where he made him an offer on the spot.

As for the other search firm, they never knew what hit them.

And as far as I know, Mike's the only account executive who ever held an EIO in his car!

This is such a rewarding business, if it's approached the right way. Hopefully, you've learned a few things from *Billing Power!*

And hopefully, you'll learn the terrific feeling that comes from being a Ninja recruiter!

About the Author

BILL RADIN began his career in executive search in 1985, after receiving his masters degree from the University of Southern California.

As a specialist in the permanent placement of electrical engineers, Bill quickly established himself as a top-producing recruiter and department manager, serving the needs of a wide range of client companies, including such multinational giants as Mobil Oil, TRW, Westinghouse and Emerson Electric.

Under his leadership as training director, Bill helped Search West of Los Angeles and Management Recruiters of Cincinnati set individual and company billing records.

By combining years of practical recruiting and management experience with modern selling technology, Bill's innovative training methods have helped produce dramatic, measurable performance improvements in both new and experienced recruiters.

He is the founder of Innovative Consulting, a company dedicated to the growth and development of the executive search industry, and continues his full-time search activities as president of Radin Associates.

Bill Radin resides in Cincinnati, Ohio with his wife Ruth.

Index

Also by Bill Radin

Each Career Development Report is an eight-page candidate training booklet, formatted as a legal-sized (8.5 x 14) camera-ready master that you can print (high-quality photocopier or offset) in any quantity desired. The masters are yours to keep, and can be customized with your logo and printed on any type paper you wish. Topics include:

Overcoming the Fear of Change
How to Construct a Dynamite Resume
How to Master the Art of Interviewing
Seven Keys to Interview Preparation
Position Comparison: How to Evaluate a Job Offer
The Proper Way to Resign
Executive Recruiters: Your Job-Search Commandos

"The *Reports* should be read by every mid- to upper-level executive interested in landing a new position."

--- Nancy Schretter, Publisher
The Search Bulletin

Also by Bill Radin

The Recruiter's ALMANAC of Scripts, Rebuttals and Closes

Bill Radin

"Great scripts for making the game of recruiting and placement easier to win."

--- Joy Perkins, Vice President
Diversified Human Resources Group, Inc.

Also by Bill Radin

"Contains specific techniques you've never heard before. A great follow-up to Billing Power!"

--- Danny Cahill
International Speaker/Trainer

ORDER FORM
Books and Tapes
by Bill Radin

Please rush:

___ copies *Billing Power!* @ $49.95 $ _____

___ copies *The Recruiter's Almanac* @ $49.95 $ _____

___ copies *Shut Up & Make More Money* @ $49.95 $ _____

___ copies *Career Development Reports* @ $49.95 $ _____

___ copies *Recruiting & The Art of Control* @ $195.00 $ _____

         Subtotal $ _____

         Less 15% for orders of 3 or more products $ _____

         Add $5.00 shipping & handling $ _____

         GRAND TOTAL $ _____

Name _____

Company _____

Street _____

City _____ State _____

Zip _____ Telephone _____

Payment: ____ Check ____ Visa/MC ____ Discover ____ AMEX

Card number _____ Exp. _____

Signature _____

Call toll-free or fax to: (800) 837-7224 • Fax: (513) 624-7502

Or send to: INNOVATIVE CONSULTING, INC.
                          5769 Eaglesridge Lane
                          Cincinnati, Ohio 45230